HOW TO CHANGE YOUR LIFE WITH JUST ONE THOUGHT

Energy medicine tools to help you release limiting beliefs
for a life full of abundance, health, love and happiness

DR. TONI CAMACHO

BALBOA.
PRESS
A DIVISION OF HAY HOUSE

Balboa Press books may be ordered through booksellers or by contacting:

Balboa Press
A Division of Hay House
1663 Liberty Drive
Bloomington, IN 47403
www.balboapress.com
1 (877) 407-4847

Print information available on the last page.

ISBN: 978-1-9822-3226-9 (sc)
ISBN: 978-1-9822-3228-3 (hc)
ISBN: 978-1-9822-3227-6 (e)

Library of Congress Control Number: 2019911181

Balboa Press rev. date: 08/05/2019

CONTENTS

PART 4
Emotions

PART 5
Understanding Your Subconscious

PART 6
Encouraging Positive Energy Flow: Eliminating Limiting Beliefs and Energy Blocks

PART 7
How to Use Energy Medicine

INTRODUCTION

"You are what you think about all day long," Dr. Wayne Dyer often said. That's because he knew that everything in your life is a result of what and how you think. Everything—health, people, events, and relationships—is a reflection of your predominant thoughts.

Have you ever wondered where your thoughts come from? They don't just pop into your mind out of thin air; they come from your subconscious, based on the beliefs that you formed throughout your lifetime (or lifetimes). The subconscious is a repository of endless thoughts, memories, and experiences; most of them, you are not even aware of.

Think of it like a file cabinet, a place where you store and organize information for future use. The contents of your file cabinet come from DNA, life experiences, obstacles you've tackled, family beliefs, where you've lived, etc. Just like a file cabinet, your subconscious doesn't care what you put in it; its job is to hold stuff as you process it. However, depending on yours and your family's life experiences, your file cabinet can be full of either useful resources or junk.

The subconscious uses this repository of information to direct all your life experiences—from what food you like to eat to the activities you do each day, the level of income you receive, and even how you react to stressful situations. In other words, your subconscious beliefs and interpretations guide every aspect of your life. Therefore, what you are experiencing at this moment is the culmination of everything you believe.

Our belief system is very complex; it was created in part by our ancestral inheritance, and the rest we picked up from our life experiences, family, and other caretakers. Some of these beliefs are unconscious and some are conscious, and they act as the software that runs our personalities and determines our behaviors and circumstances. Therefore, if you want to experience a different situation in your life, you need to change the subconscious belief that created it. This may be harder than it sounds, since most of our beliefs are unconscious; in other words, we are unaware of them. Therefore, it makes it almost impossible to make changes by using only our intellect.

Unfortunately, for every conscious thought that we have, one million subconscious thoughts are going on without us being aware. Furthermore, research by Benjamin Lebit demonstrated that consciousness does not even have an active, executive role in determining behavior. Instead, our sense of making choices or decisions is just an awareness of what the subconscious has already decided for us. The fact is when we become aware of our subconscious actions, we think about them and falsely conclude that our intentions have caused them [1].

Moreover, according to Professor Guy Claxton at Oxford University, no intention or plan is ever conceived in consciousness. Libet's experiments showed that brain activity appears a fifth of a second before a person has the conscious thought or intention to act. In other words, something is telling us what to do before we think we need to do it. Therefore, the belief that we are making conscious choices is all an illusion; the reality is that every thought comes directed from our subconscious [2].

In other words, the urge to act, such as when we choose to get a cup of coffee, may seem like a conscious choice to you, but the reality is that your subconscious based on your beliefs is the one that gave you the instruction to get the cup of coffee. Your conscious mind, rationalizing your action, came up with the intention of "A cup of coffee will be nice now. So I go will make a coffee." Ultimately, you could also have chosen not to have a cup of coffee. However, you would have found a different way to rationalize your choice. Regardless of your choice, according to Lebit, you could not control the origin of the signal that was nudging you to act [1].

Your subconscious mind is composed of all your life experiences. That includes everything anyone has said to you, and all you have read, heard, or seen. All this content forms a filter of belief through which you will interpret and create everything in your life. As a consequence, you are always explaining and shaping your life through the screen of your beliefs. What you believe produces a unique representation of the world and runs your thoughts, judgments, pleasures, and your troubles. Consequently, you are continually modifying what you see and experience according to what you believe. It is a genuine experience, yet it is only real for you and no one else.

As a result, real change can happen only when you change the limiting beliefs about yourself and the world that are in your subconscious. What you think, feel, and do, not only impacts your physical body, it also affects and changes the frequency of our energetic anatomy. Our energetic anatomy is a field of energy composed of many interconnected layers that are in and around our physical body. The frequency of this energy is what attracts circumstances and life events that match that vibration into your life. High vibration attracts what we call favorable conditions, and low vibrations attract unfavorable situations. This vibration gets generated by the quality of the food we eat, our beliefs, thoughts we think, emotions we feel, and environment we are exposed to.

My goal for this book is to empower you with energy medicine tools that can help you reprogram or overwrite the limiting or damaging beliefs stored in your subconscious mind, so you can release energetic blocks and create a healthier and happier life. As well as to help you learn the real power behind your beliefs so that you can see how you can create the life you choose.

I am a nutritionist, holistic health practitioner, Reiki Master, and Doctor of Psychology. I am also a registered clinical herbalist and have been professionally trained on how to design and make herbal medicine. I started my inner journey twenty five years ago. Like many others, I had experienced mixed results trying to change what was outside of me, buying into the myth that I would be ok once I had this, or when I found that. This search took me to many different teachers and healing modalities. Therefore, many schools of thought and mentors have influenced me. My training includes Eastern and Western nutrition, herbology, energy medicine, Tibetan Buddhist and clinical psychology, and a certified Jack Canfield success coach (Law of Attraction coach).

How to change your life with just one thought is based on my energy medicine training and experience, as well as the techniques that I have applied successfully throughout the years, while working with many clients in clinic. This book is also broadly influenced by both classical and contemporary philosophy, as well as deeply rooted in both Western and Eastern ancient wisdom.

In my practice as a counselor and coach, I often assist and support people who are motivated to change what's holding them back. I help them identify where they want to go and how to get there. Usually, coaching focuses on what is real now, in the present moment, and what actions need to be taken to produce results. However, I have found that mapping out plans and acting is only one part of the puzzle. And many times, working from the details creates controlled solutions without the underlying problem ever being resolved. Therefore, focusing on what people believe is more important than problem-solving. Since to produce lasting and positive change, people need to change what they believe so they can address the root of the problem.

This book starts with a look at what beliefs are, where they come from, how they determine what you experience, and the impact they have on our relationships. Since beliefs affect our energetic anatomy, I also spend time explaining what and how the components of your energetic anatomy, such as the aura, chakras, and meridians, work and how they interact with our physical body to form your consciousness and create your current circumstances.

The entire essence of this book can be summed up in Buddha's quote: "To enjoy good health, to bring true happiness to one's family, to bring peace to all, one must first discipline and control one's own mind. If a man can control his mind, he can find the way to Enlightenment, and all wisdom and virtue will naturally come to him." Know that you do not need gurus, psychics, teachers, or masters to reach peace, happiness, and health—your life is in your hands. You are an expression of the divine, and as such, you have been given at birth the same power of creation; all you must do is believe.

PART 1
Who Are You?

Only those who see that the two sides of all phenomena,
visible and invisible, or front and back or beginning
and end of one reality can embrace any antagonistic
situation, see its complementarity, and help others to do
the same, thereby establishing peace and harmony.
— George Ohsawa

CHAPTER 1

The Components of Your Consciousness

> We are the cosmos made conscious and life is the
> means by which the universe understands itself.
> — Brian Cox

We all know that we have a physical body, but what most people do not know is that we also have a light body—a timeless, energetic essence that connects us to everything in the universe; this is often referred to as our energetic anatomy or energetic body. **Together your physical body and energy anatomy form your consciousness.** One is not more important or more spiritual than the other; both are needed for our growth and development. In fact, Max Planck, a physicist who originated quantum theory, regarded "consciousness as fundamental" and matter as a "derivative from consciousness."

I want to emphasize that the physical body is as essential as the spirit, otherwise one would not be in his or her body. I know this strikes a chord for many people, since some interpretations of spiritual traditions emphasize leaving this planet and letting go of the Ego as a priority or a way to reach Nirvana.

However, creation does not make mistakes. If you are here, it is because you are meant to be here for your development. Judging your experience does not bring you closer to Nirvana or Enlightenment. Even the Buddha said, "If a man can control his mind, he can find the way to Enlightenment, and all wisdom and virtue will naturally come to him."

The fact is that what you resist persist and the more you reject and judge your current existence, the more you will get stuck in it. It is far more comfortable and more productive to accept "what is." Acceptance is being open to the moment to moment experience of life and being willing to feel without trying to control it. Let's use as an example the hobby of cloud watching. During this exercise, you probably don't get upset that the clouds are not forming into the specific shapes you want or think that they should be someplace better. Instead, there is no resistance to the moment to moment experience; there is only observation and acceptance.

We are also not meant to wrestle with or to try to eliminate our Ego. Contrary to popular belief, our Ego is neither good nor bad. The Ego is part of our consciousness; it is merely the part of us that responds to our surroundings and gives a specific experience (perception or interpretation). In other words, every experience you have is filtered through your Ego, which frames it based on your subconscious beliefs. Your Ego decides if what you are experiencing is good or bad. That is to say, something is right for us because the Ego interprets it as is true.

The Ego also takes your beliefs and turns them into reality through our energetic anatomy. Our energetic anatomy is composed of several parts. You may have heard of some of them, such as the aura, chakras, nadis, kundalini, and **meridians,** amongst others.

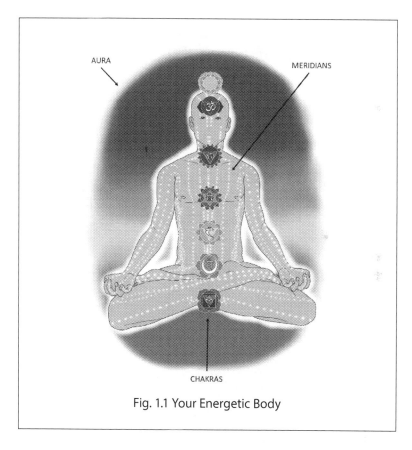

Fig. 1.1 Your Energetic Body

All parts of your consciousness—physical or not—are interconnected, and they interact and affect each other, as well as occupy the same space. If one component changes, it affects and changes the rest.

The transmission of energy through these systems is bidirectional. Energy flowing through the meridians gathers information from your cells and emotions and then is transferred in the form of energy to the chakras. The chakras translate this and send all the information collected to the aura, where it gets radiated outward, relaying the quality and vibration of your being. In other words, the energy patterns in your aura are the result of the programs (beliefs) in your subconscious mind in the form of energy.

You interact with different dimensions and realities through the energy of the aura, since it radiates the quality and vibration of your being as a frequency. These realities and dimensions also have a frequency. Like energy attracts like energy. Therefore, this frequency is what attracts to your experience the reality that matches your vibration.

Likewise, frequency coming down the aura gets passed down to the chakras, where this information gets translated to a level that the physical body can assimilate. Chakras move the energy to the meridians, and the meridians make the energy available to your physical body and mind.

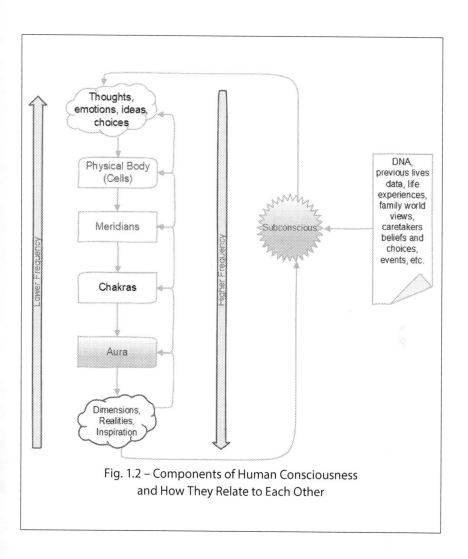

Fig. 1.2 – Components of Human Consciousness
and How They Relate to Each Other

Through meditation and other forms of energy medicine, the aura can consciously be programed to attract specific things, people, and events. The strength and state of your aura will determine the strength of your attraction and the kind of events, people, and things that you attract in your life.

In the rest of this book, I will explore each of the components of consciousness in detail, starting with our beliefs, since these are what originally dictated our thoughts, emotions, choices, and ideas, which end up being part of our aura. Therefore, they are the source of our life conditions. This is based on the premise that nothing exists outside of us that we did not create; everything we experience has been created by our beliefs about ourselves and the world, and as such, we have been given the power to change it by changing the mindset that created it. This means you are 100 percent responsible for your health, your life, and the behavior of everyone in it. There is no more blaming our genes, age, your mom, your kids, pesticides, mercury retrograde, astrological sign, cell towers, and so on. Taking responsibility for your life is not about making you feel bad, guilt, or punishment. Instead, it is about empowering you to take back control of your life. There is no need to judge or criticize yourself for your current circumstances. Know that you are always doing the best you can with the limited awareness and beliefs that you have in that moment.

It is very critical for you to be aware that if you could have done better in the past, you would have. All the shoulda, coulda, woulda in your head are your ego's way to protect you from the fear of facing something different, something outside your familiar zone. Unfortunately, if you continue to focus intensely on the past - even if you do not want to, it increases the probability that you will experience and behave in the same manner again.

The only positive purpose of guilt is the awareness it brings you of how your past actions are not in alignment with your current beliefs. Therefore, you don't have to dwell on the past; instead, use this awareness to make new and improve choices that will create a new reality that aligns with what you want.

Until you can honestly accept and say, "I have a choice in what happens in my health and my life. I am in this place now because of the choices I've made and the beliefs from my past," you will not be able to say, "I will make different choices." You got yourself consciously or unconsciously into your current situation, and you can get out of it by taking responsibility for your life and making the changes to attract the life circumstances you desire.

These changes can happen at any one of the levels discussed earlier—for example, you can change your life by changing what you eat or unblock chakras through meditation or with flower essences. These changes may not only heal your life, but they may also trigger the necessary changes in beliefs that created the situation to begin with. However, if you do not embrace these new beliefs, you will once more attract similar circumstances into your life.

PART 2
The Only Limits We Have are The Limits We Believe

We do not see things are they are, but as we are ourselves.
— Henry Thomason

CHAPTER 2

What You Think and the Beliefs You Hold Determine What You Experience

It's what you choose to believe that
makes you the person you are.
— Karen Marie Moning

Research reveals we are active contributors to everything we see in the world around us. In physics, the term "observer effect" relates to the alterations that the act of observation makes to the properties of what is observed. Quantum physics states that no phenomenon exists until it is observed. In other words, until something has been observed, it will not show up into the physical world. In fact, Eugene Wigner, a theoretical physicist and mathematician, stressed how "it was not possible to formulate the laws of quantum mechanics in a fully consistent way without reference to consciousness." [3]

For example, prominent researchers Robert Jahn and Brenda Dunne performed an experiment involving an RMC (random mechanical cascade) machine in the form of a big pinball machine fixed on the wall, which dropped balls from the center and let them bounce over an arrangement of pegs. The balls typically ended up in the center, but sometimes they landed far to one side. The experiment asked the human subjects to sit in front of the machine and "think right" or "think left." Jahn and Dunne noted that deviations from the RMC's normal distribution matched with the conscious intentions of the test subjects much more often than one would have expected randomly [4].

Jahn also explored the ability of test subjects to influence the random output distribution of a quantum random event generator (REG). The research provided highly statistically significant evidence that the effects being observed, though small in magnitude, were not merely chance. With the probability that this could occur by chance was less than one in a million [5].

Similarly, other studies have demonstrated that the intentions of a group of people—particularly expert meditators—have a stronger and more coherent impact on the behavior of these random number generators [6]. Likewise, other research studies have shown that meditators are able to collapse quantum systems at a distance through intention alone [7]. The researchers concluded that "Observations not only disturb what has to be measured, they produce it ... We compel [the electron] to assume a definite position ... We ourselves produce the results of measurement." [8]

Additional longitudinal studies showed that the intention of a large group of advanced meditators, in fact, influence social behavior, such as reducing crime rates and decreased violence.

In these studies, researchers asked experienced meditators to focus on reducing crime in the US. Rigorous statistical analysis found a significant decrease, 21.2% over four years (5.3% per year) in both the national homicide rate and urban violent crime rate compared to trends during the baseline period of the study. Researchers concluded that approximately 8,157 homicides were prevented due to the significant shift from an increasing to a decreasing trend in homicide rates. [9]

"such research is increasingly suggesting that there's a field effect of consciousness. If you get a large enough group together practicing this technique to experience the field quality of consciousness, these extended 'field-like' effects are expressed in society," stated co-author Dr. Michael Dillbeck. [9]

Likewise, French scientist Rene Peoc'h tested the possible influence of eighty groups of fifteen chicks on a small, randomly moving robot. On hatching, the chicks were exposed to the robot, for them to become "imprinted" onto the robot. In the first part of the experiment, the robot was set to move around in a room that was empty, except for an empty cage on one side of the room. The result was as expected: the robot followed a random trajectory. In the second part of the experiment, Peoc'h placed the chicks in the cage and then put the robot in the room as before. This time the robot stayed in the half of the room where the chicks were, especially directly in front of the cage. In 71 percent of the cases, the robot spent an excessive amount of time in the proximity of the chicks. In the absence of the chicks, the robot followed random trajectories. Concluding that, even the rudimentary consciousness of chicks was able to influence the robot's behavior. [10]

These experiments are just a few of countless tests that have confirmed the active role of human intention (consciousness) in the establishment of physical reality. And since our subconscious guides our perceptions of what is being observed based on our beliefs, **we cannot help but take part in shaping the events and circumstances in our lives**. Our consciousness affects everything from the cells in our bodies to the world we live in.

Our intention is made up of the energy of our thoughts, feelings, and emotions, and these, in turn, are directed by our subconscious, based on our beliefs about ourselves and the world. How we think determines our feelings and behaviors, and our behaviors shape the quality of our lives. For that reason, anything that we experience in our lives is a result of what and how we think.

Reality, however, is created not only by the intent of the observer but also by the collective observers. Therefore, if you are not consciously creating your own life (with focused intention), other people, like your significant other, boss, kids, parents, or spiritual leaders, will do it for you. When it comes to shared experiences, as seen in the group meditation experiments, whoever has the most active (focused) intention has more impact on the outcome. For that reason, your reality and actions at any given moment are always a reflection of the current state of your mind and the predominant collective consciousness.

Moreover, our thoughts, feelings, and emotions are expressions of energy that send out signals about our expectations and beliefs of reality. We live in a pliable world, where everything is continually changing to match our beliefs. How long this experience will last or how much it will affect you will depend on your perception of how much weight, impact, and energy an issue has in your life. The more you obsess, reject, or resist "what is," the more it will persist.

Likewise, since energy responds to our mental and emotional focus, it tends to follow the same pattern over and over, just as our thoughts do. As we get stuck repeating the same conscious and subconscious thoughts without changing our beliefs, the same energetic configuration occurs, creating the same living conditions we continuously experience.

Through our beliefs, we hold the ability to change our lives, our bodies, and the world by choice. Improving our lives, relationships, and bodies requires a precise yet straightforward shift in what we believe.

CHAPTER 3

We're Only Limited by What We Think of Ourselves and the World

Man is what he believes.
— Anton Chekhov

The way you experience the circumstances in your life is based on thousands of beliefs you have formulated throughout your life (and previous lives) about you and your relationship with the world. People often suffer unpleasant or undesirable, feelings, situations, and circumstances, without knowing how they participate in creating or recreating their experiences. What most people don't know is that what they consistently think about (a dominant thought) and how they think about it eventually shows up into existence.

Most of what we think, say, or do is generated by something that we have heard, seen, or done in the past. In fact, scientists speculate that about **99 percent of what our brain perceives around us is based on what is already present in our minds**. According to Dr. Emmanuel Donchin, director of the laboratory for cognitive psychophysiology at the University of Illinois, "an enormous portion of cognitive activity is nonconscious. We probably will never know precisely how much is outside of our awareness." [11]

One of the best-known experiments in psychology that demonstrates how our intuition deceives us and how much is around us that we don't see is the invisible gorilla experiment. This experiment was carried out at Harvard University. In this study, subjects were asked to watch a video of six people passing a basketball, three in white shirts and three in black shirts. While they watched, subjects were asked to count the number of times the ball was passed by the people in the white shirts. During the video, a gorilla walks in the middle of the action, faces the camera, and thumps its chest. The gorilla is visible for nine seconds, but over half the people watching the video don't notice it, as though the gorilla is invisible to them. *The gorilla passes right through the zone of attention and isn't noticed.* [12]

This experiment reveals that we often are missing a lot of what goes on around us, and more importantly that we have no idea how much we are missing. [12] For instance, a simple but practical example of this is the times when you are looking for your missing keys, cell phone, or sunglasses. You look everywhere, such as under the couch, in the car, on the counter, in your purse, your pants, on the floor. You keep looking until someone tells you that you have them in your hands! or in the case of the sunglasses on your head! Because you "believe" even for a moment that you have lost the item, you have eliminated the possibility that you had them in your hands. Just because of this **short term belief**, your senses (sight, tastes, sound, smell, and touch) did not allow the information to be perceived, denying the obvious.

We usually assess what we experience based on what we know, your beliefs will determine how you interpret the information you absorb moment to moment, and this may cause us to easily overlook something positive that is in front of us. In other words, **if you do not believe it, you won't see it!** An event can be happening in front of you (like a gorilla thumping its chest), yet you won't allow it into your perception until you accept it as a possibility by challenging and expanding your limits. Until there is real acceptance with anything in life, the mind can't and won't give meaning and action to the event at hand. Inevitably, not changing our beliefs causes us to miss opportunities.

As you can see, with experiments like the invisible gorilla, science is now validating what sages like Buddha said over thousands of years ago: a person's life is shaped subconsciously, and we create our reality based on our beliefs.

The brain stores information from our experiences to gives us a frame of reference of whom and what we are. The brain also takes these data and creates a structure for how to interpret the future. Unfortunately, this structure is not the best framework for us in cases when we had a dysfunctional or painful past because it limits us to what we believe is possible. Consequently, the only way to be, do, and have something different than you currently have is to retrain your subconscious mind.

Positive beliefs are rarely a problem. It is the negative ones, usually acquired early in life, that cause people to feel stuck or suffer. When we are focused consciously or unconsciously on a traumatic experience or unpleasant thoughts, the energy of these thoughts becomes dominant and creates negative feelings. If we focus regularly on negative thought patterns, we are unconsciously fueling our cells with negative energy that will not only define our behavior and expectations of how the world functions but also attract what we do not want in our lives.

Therefore, **whatever limits you set for yourself in relationship with the world are the ones you will experience**. Know for sure that if you do not believe you have specific skills or abilities or if you believe you do not deserve something, your subconscious mind will work to confirm your belief mentally, verbally, and physically. Look at your subconscious beliefs as the seeds that contain what **you intend to be** each day.

Having a belief does not automatically create the reality to match your beliefs; it does, however, give you the faith needed to take the necessary steps to realize it. **A great paradox is that you will always seek validation of what you believe about yourself and the world**. No matter if you think you are dumb, smart, peaceful, good, or bad, someone that does not matter or someone that is loved, you will seek to prove your beliefs at all costs. Your subconscious and conscious will act when needed to confirm a belief about yourself and the world that is not currently reflecting or is challenging a belief. By focusing on what you believe yourself to be, you alter and shape the content of your life until it matches the exact belief. What we call the self-fulling prophecy is nothing but the results of the memories in your subconscious.

Know that **your subconscious and conscious will go to any lengths to accomplish the goal of self-validation!** You will rationalize it, justify it, accept it, condemn it, or change your outer circumstances until you get confirmation of its existence. Remember that what you focus on expands. We spend a lot of energy, keeping up with stories that may or may not be valid. And we will collect evidence so we can easily justify them. Why this is possible, and that is impossible. Why this will work, and that will never work. Why I get along with her and why I can't get along with him. Why things always end up this way. In the end, our fixation with interpreting and defining everything significantly constrains our ability to see what is happening.

We do this because the boundaries of what we know keep us safe. Even if we are currently suffering, what we know explains everything. It helps us understand who we are and what we can and cannot do. We go as far as making up a narrative to support the interpretation of what is happening and how everything is. We become so invested in our story; that we will protect it at any cost. Unfortunately, we see what we want to see according to what we believe, and it keeps us from seeing what is real.

The desire to put everything into the boundaries of what we know is powerful. So much that some people go as far as dying or killing to prove their beliefs and resolve the incongruence between their belief and what they are currently experiencing. But we do not have to go to these extremes; we can see it in everyday life as people change jobs, end relationships, or move to a different city just to avoid what is causing them pain or discomfort. However, in the end, they find themselves experiencing the same uncomfortable feeling, but now with a new lover, in a new city, or at a new job, all because they did not realize that everything in front of them is nothing but a reflection of themselves. Nothing exists "out there." It's in *you*.

Undesired states of mind and feelings result from holding on to limiting beliefs about who you are and the world around you. And you will experience over and over the same situations or feelings until you get tired of this dynamic and begin to change your view (belief). *Changing or avoiding the external circumstances that are causing you pain only suppresses the real issue* because it does not allow you to pay attention to the underlying belief causing the pain. Instead, your approach should be to become aware of the source of your belief, process the experience from the past, and create yourself a new belief and consequently a new reality.

CHAPTER 4

Beliefs and Our Relationships

The people we are in relationship with are always a mirror, reflecting our own beliefs, and simultaneously we are mirrors reflecting their beliefs. So, relationship is one of the most powerful tools for growth ... if we look honestly at our relationships, we can see so much about how we have created them.
— Shakti Gawain

The meaning we give to people in our lives, whether positive or negative, is always brought about and composed by our dominant and subconscious thoughts and beliefs. These are created by how people around us reacted to events throughout our lives and get recorded into our subconscious mind to later become the blueprint of how we deal with relationships.

Since **90 percent or more of our daily actions are responses that come from information accumulated during the first seven years of our life,** it makes sense that most of our adult relationships are mirroring our primary caretakers' reactions to how they saw the world and what they told us about ourselves

[13]. Our bonding patterns (the normal and natural way in which we give and receive nurturance) are also very similar to those that we had in our past with our parents, siblings, and other main caretakers. We literally recreate our history, or we do the opposite and rebel against it, creating the opposite experience. To a certain degree, this is natural behavior – but in certain situations, it is no longer rewarding. Therefore, these bonding patterns are often the primary reason for the disintegration of the feelings of love in a relationship and are often responsible for the destruction of a positive sexual experience. [14] Such is the case when the mother or father in us, relates to the child in our spouse. And conversely, the child in us relates to the mother or father in our spouse. There are many ways and combinations in which this pattern can show up; I won't look at them all here. Nevertheless, here is an example of an unhealthy bounding pattern:

Helen tends to play the caretaker "mother" role in her relationships, particularly with men. This caretaking part of herself "bonds in" with her husband's Ryan's unspoken needs. When her "default behavior" takes over, she feels she must take care of Ryan and his unspoken feelings. Even if she does not take care of herself – a role she habitually assumes with men. As this happens, Ryan's default behavior kicks in, and he becomes more and more rational in his response and separates more and more from his feelings. Consequently, he becomes the thinker and planner in the relationship - and he is the responsible, stoic, well-organized father, a role he regularly assumes with women. This type of interaction allows them both to have access to modes of expression of the selves they disowned and previously didn't have access to.

If we pay attention to this bonding pattern, we can see that the mother part of Helen is taking care of the son part of Ryan while the father part of Ryan is taking care of the daughter part of Helen. Because of this, neither of them brings the fullness of themselves to the other. Ryan can't feel his feelings, and Helen does not use her intelligence. This type of relationship works for a while. However, as soon as stress occurs, for instance, if Ryan has a bad day, the attraction to the disowned self in the other person converts into judgment. Your defenses kick in, and your basic selves become dominant again. You then judge what is unlike you in your partner.

Regardless of if we duplicate the relationship with our early caretakers or rebel against it, every relationship reflects our thoughts, beliefs, and feelings about ourselves. Therefore, we always attract to us the people and relationships that will provide us with the opportunity to reconnect with a part of us; this happens at a subconscious level. We may not be able to see these beliefs in ourselves. But we can see how these beliefs impact our lives by looking at how we treat others. Also in the behaviors towards us of the people in our most intimate romantic relationships, friendships, and family. Every person and relationship we have in our life is mirroring our conscious and subconscious beliefs and the relationship we have with ourselves. [15]

How and what we perceive in our relationships reflect both our positive and negative patterns. Including patterns such as the rescuer, the mother, the hero, the child, etc. However, the most common and loudest patterns that we encounter are the ones associated with the voices of the "judge" or the "victim." The judge is the voice in our head that comments on how things should be such as "you/they are doing it wrong,"

"You should be ashamed," "they/you should be punished," "they/you should act like this or like that." In other words, the critic argues for the rules about what is supposed to be wrong and right. The judge is also the perfectionist in us, the one that no matter how we do things, or what we do and achieve, is never good enough.

On the other hand, is the victim, the victim listens and accepts what the judge says, and its dialog goes something like "it is not my fault," "no one ever listens to me," "it's not fair," "I can't help it… I'm [this or that] …", "my personality is…", "no matter what I do is never good enough." The victim often complains and makes up poor me stories. The victim also has a hard time being in the present moment, it is easier for him/her to be in the past and believes that everything will be alright if only this or that… and looks into the future and thinks everything is going to be ok when… this or that happens. This type of beliefs makes it impossible to live in the moment and to get ahead and out of the current circumstances.

Moreover, the judge and the victim in our relationships are reflecting a particular "I'm not" or "I can't" statement tied to a belief about ourselves and the world that is holding us back. Such as, I'm not good enough, I'm not smart enough, I'm not wanted, I'm not ok as I am, I can't do it right. I can't get what I want, etc.

We project all these statements on to other people. For example, an "I can't do it" narrative may be projected as a rescuing act or fall into a pattern of saving others but ignoring our own needs. Like, "I will do this for you because I don't believe you can do it." Revealing an underlying voice that says: I don't respect you enough to believe you can do it.

That's because deep down I don't think I can do it either. Our perceptions in relationships are never about anyone else. The other person is just the external trigger that is causing you to want to change something inside you.

Less than loving relationships show us a part of ourselves that we do not love and accept. [15] **Everyone in our lives is there to support our healing and help release energy that has been blocked** in our physical and energetic bodies. When a person treats us in an unloving way, it is the perfect opportunity for us to reconnect to a part of ourselves that we are withholding love from and to love and accept it the way it is. So long as we disown these parts of us, we will continue to attract people and relationships with the characteristics we disown as well as characteristics that we dislike, judge, and resent over and over. Conversely, if we genuinely love ourselves, the more we will attract harmonious, loving relationships or people with the characteristics we love and enjoy.

There is nothing more powerful than changing what you believe! Therefore, if you want to change an aspect of a relationship right now, you should not change the external circumstance. Instead, change the fundamental belief. Otherwise, you will attract the same experience but with a different person. In your new experience the people or the setting may be different but the fundamental experience, or how you felt as a result of it, will be the same.

To attract a different experience, you need to vibrate at the same rate as the new experience that you desire. However, your vibration will not align with your new desire, while you believe there is something not right or something missing from your current relationship. If you leave the relationship, you leave with the belief, sense, and vibration of lack, which in turns attracts the same situation again. Know that your vibration will change as you change your belief. And either your current relationship changes to meet your desires, or you will attract a new relationship that matches your new vibration.

There is a purpose for every single relationship we have. We come together with people to help us solve our limiting beliefs. The more difficult the relationship, the deeper the message we are being asked to receive. The pain you feel is there for a reason. It is revealing something within you that is missing, lacking or unsettled. This relationship is guiding you toward awareness and healing.

There is an unspoken energetic commitment or contract that we make with the people in our closest relationships—like in the case of our romantic partners and family members—to be in our lives and reflect us our beliefs long term. Because of the nature and duration of these relationships, they are in our lives to help us learn the lessons we have agreed to work on and intended to learn in this life, and they will be with us until we are ready to accept the truth.

Remember, everything you experience is about you and how you see the world, so once these beliefs are cleared, the issue clears up for both of you. And your relationship changes. So, instead of judging and condemning an aspect of a relationship, ask yourself what is going on within you that is expressing the perceived problem. And work on changing or clearing the belief.

The exception will be if you are in an abusive relationship or are being harmed in some way. The priority will be to put yourself out of danger and make a change to the relationship if needed. Then before starting a new relationship, work on changing the fundamental belief that created the situation; otherwise, you will repeat the same pattern with a different person.

In all other circumstances, it is not wise to expect or wish from your lover, friend, or family member a different behavior or attitude, so you can experience a better feeling. There is no need to wish your relationship was different or think that if only you met someone else, you would feel different. What you are looking at is a miracle in your life. It does not need to be anything else other than what is, or you might miss something beautiful that is hidden behind your limiting belief. What you are seeing that is making you uncomfortable is the part of you that needs healing. Change your perception and what you are looking at will transform into whatever you desire.

According to Esther Hicks, you have the power to evoke from others the relationships that you desire. But you will not get a new and improved circumstance by giving your attention to what you perceive is lacking. She states "You have the power to evoke from others a relationship that is in harmony with the freedom, and the growth, and the joy that you seek, because within each of the others are those probabilities. Within each of them is the probability of someone being very understanding—or not. Of someone being very pleasant— or not. Of someone being very open-minded—or not. Of someone being very positive—or negative. The experience that you have with others is about what you evoke from them" [16]

Instead of focusing on what's lacking in a relationship, focus on what your higher-self sees in that person. Focus on what it is that you love or like about them. And what about them you want more of. As you are willing and able to take your partner and family member as he or she is and as your love deepens for him/her, you will automatically make peace with that part of yourself, and his or her behavior will change and reflect your new belief.

Be grateful and appreciate every person in your life, for they are there to support your growth.

CHAPTER 5

Where Do Our Beliefs Come From?

Remember that what you believe will
depend very much on what you are.
— Noah Porte

All our beliefs originate from the conscious or subconscious mind, and both play a role in formulating who we are. Some of these beliefs are passed down from generation to generation. According to Margaret Ruby in her book *The DNA of Healing*, an emotional history has been handed down to us through our lineage. How we react to others, the way we communicate, the way we think and express our emotions, and even the patterns of our relationships, health, and finances are shaped by our genes. The feelings and beliefs of our ancestors are locked deep in the memory of our DNA. [17]

Additionally, scientific research has proven that a woman's psychological states and emotional propensities during pregnancy influence their children. [18] Children can take on the mental and emotional experiences of the mother while in the womb. These tendencies can include low self-esteem, self-value, and self-worth. Therefore, some of the feelings people are experiencing in their lives may have nothing to do with them [19] [20]. Instead, a person might be reacting to beliefs, thoughts, and feelings that they picked up from their mother while they were in the womb. For example, if the child is the result of an unwanted pregnancy (mom's experience), he/she can grow up with an inherited belief of low self-worth.

Other beliefs we take on throughout our life. People have a long list of beliefs about themselves and the world based on the stories they heard or made up in reaction to the life experiences they had. Therefore, some of what they believe is composed of long-forgotten agreements they've made with themselves in response to the adverse events they experienced. For example, "I do not deserve positive attention from others," "I am uncreative," "people are out to get whatever they can from you," "I always end up being used." Unfortunately, an agreement grows stronger through reinforcement and repetition. Even though each of our experiences has taken place only once, we may have re-lived them a thousand times in our minds. Making them thousands of times more powerful. Additionally, other times, incidents repeat in many different forms all carrying the same general message; therefore, they become strong beliefs.

Often, the most disruptive beliefs begin early in life. These beliefs are formed in childhood based on what is seen, heard and were led to believe about who they are and how the world is. [13] Studies have shown that until age seven, our brains are in a dreamlike state, where our minds are absorbing everything that is happening around us. During these years, we soak up information about us and the world without any filters to tell us what is wrong or what is right. (13) It is all information that **we register in our subconscious**. During this time, we let other people's experiences create our own template without any discernment. Therefore, the beliefs of others become the foundation of what we believe true about the world and ourselves. These are the things we later in life recognize as judgments, biases, likes, and dislikes. Sometimes these beliefs stay through our entire lives, and other times we change as we process beliefs and grow.

Scientists estimate that about 95 percent of daily actions are directed from a subconscious level. (13) The subconscious mind is larger and five hundred thousand times faster than the conscious mind. (21) The subconscious works fast and instinctively without thoughts and considerations to slow it down. This is great when needing to run away from a tiger or letting our bodies breathe on their own. This is not such a great thing when we automatically react to others' behaviors or life events, especially when we are responding based on our limiting belief or unhealthy patterns we learned in childhood.

Because these reactions are unconscious, it is challenging to see them in ourselves; we might not even be able to see them when we act them out, even when it is pretty evident to those around us. Have you ever been offended when a loved one told you that you are acting just like your mother or father? Have you denied it or said they are crazy? You don't see it because it is a subconscious action. However, you can see them, if you pay attention and become aware of your life circumstances and your relationships, since they reflect what is in both your conscious and subconscious mind.

Your subconscious mind has a record of everything that you have ever experienced. Our bodies also contain our histories, everything that has happened to us. It also keeps a cross-reference log of how we felt and what we felt during each event. Every situation has left an imprint in our consciousness and our bodies. Every event, relationship, thought, success, illness, failure, childhood trauma, and critical life change has been linked to our subconscious beliefs and traveled through the body, activating a physiological response.

"The emotions from these experiences become encoded in our biological systems," says Carolyn Myss [22], contributing to the formation of our cells and becoming stored in our cellular memory. The degree of importance a belief has for us depends on the feeling behind the belief; this feeling is what gives the belief its power. Therefore, **our beliefs are profound feeling experiences** that have a direct impact on the way we perceive the world.

Some of these beliefs are positive, and some of them are negative. The negative beliefs are the ones responsible for the challenging circumstances in our lives. For example, children learn during their first three years of their lives whether they can trust that they will be cared for and are safe, and this gets stored in their subconscious mind. The way adult caretakers react to children has a tremendous influence on the formation of these beliefs. The child cannot be fooled by words or by reason because he or she responds directly by feelings, so the slightest indication of disapproval or abandonment will trigger feelings and beliefs of fear and unsafety. These subconscious beliefs are triggered in affected children once they grow up, by situations that are similar to and closely aligned with the experience they had as children. However, if the person does not understand the energy that is coming from their subconscious mind, they will turn what they think and feel into self-destructive beliefs that will bring about unfavorable circumstances into their lives.

The subconscious mind also stores the content and emotions you are experiencing when watching the news, films, and television programs and reading books— basically everything that you are exposed to. The reason being is the subconscious mind does not seem to distinguish real from imaginary.

A study was done to illustrate this, where volunteers were asked to play the piano each day for five consecutive days. Their brains were scanned each day, in the region connected to the finger muscles. Another set of subjects were asked to imagine playing the notes instead, also having their brains scanned each day. The results showed the changes in the brain in those who imagined playing the piano were the same as in those who played the piano. They concluded that **what you imagine to be happening is happening, as far as your brain is concerned.** [23]

Another study looking at brain patterns in weightlifters found that the patterns activated when a weightlifter lifted hundreds of pounds were similarly activated when they only imagined lifting. [24] Moreover, Guang Yue, an exercise psychologist from Cleveland Clinic Foundation in Ohio, compared "people who went to the gym with people who carried out virtual workouts in their heads." He found that the group of subjects who conducted mental exercises of the weight training increased muscle strength by almost half as much (13.5 percent) as those who went to the gym (30 percent). [25] Therefore, it seems that whatever you are experiencing, whether it is real or imagined, is stored by the subconscious mind as an event that is real, consequently forming beliefs based on them—and shaping your life!

CHAPTER 6

To Change Your Life, You Must First Change Your Beliefs

You can do a thing only if you have
the belief that it can be done.
— Anonymous

According to Dr. Hew Len, only three states of mind exist. The first one is the way it was when you were *first* created (empty/nothing)—what Joe Vitale calls the zero point, the beginning [26]. The *second* state happens right at birth, and it is the state of inspiration—direct connection to spirit. This is where we always want to be and where our creation is to come from. After our birth, the third state of mind begins and is based on your memories and beliefs; for most of us this is where we mostly spend our time living and creating from.

Our beliefs are what's between us and inspiration. However, the more you clear your limiting beliefs, the more time you can spend on the state of inspiration and create your reality from there. Clearing beliefs about yourself and how you see the world is not an easy job. Your Ego created your sense of who you are, based on a structure made of all your experiences, memories, thoughts, stories (beliefs). This structure created what you "know," about yourself and the world. It also has shaped your life, and it plays an integral part in how you interpret everything that comes your way. Consequently, your beliefs generate a series of filters by which you perceive and create your life.

The only reason the Ego created this structure is to provide a frame of reference that helps you interpret what is happening in your life so you can feel safe. The way our minds work is that if almost everything in our lives can be explained and then understood within the borders of what we "know," we feel safe. The irony is that it does not matter if some of these ideas may work well for us or not. Assessing everything within our beliefs makes the world to us feel familiar and consequently safe.

We create our lives mostly from the third state of mind (from memories and belief). Therefore, your life circumstances and what you do is a response to what you consciously and subconsciously believe; we can only perceive the world based on the beliefs that are within us. In other words, **there's nothing "out there." It's all inside you.** That's what's causing you experience problems, and that's where the change needs to be—as Einstein said, "You cannot solve a problem with the same consciousness that created it." Everything that you believe will come back to you in the form of circumstances, illnesses, people, and other life events. You will experience life based on your limiting beliefs until the beliefs are surrendered to their false nature.

The only way out of the suffering is to accept the truth about yourself and what the situation is offering you. After this, your experience of life can change instantly. The more you clear yourself of this programming, the more you can live from a place of inspiration instead of the past.

As a result, a key to change your life and experiences is for you to be aware of how you create your unique perception of your life and the world. Without this awareness, you will not accurately experience what is in front of you. Instead, you will view an image made by the filter of your beliefs.

To transform your life, you need to be aware of what you believe and to step out of the area of what you "know." In other words, to clearly see the barriers created by what you think about yourself and the world. To be aware is to become the observer of your life — an observer with a specific purpose – to seek. What you are seeking for is the limiting beliefs that are no longer serving you and are creating the obstacles keeping you from being as happy and prosperous as you want to be.

As a human being, you always can change your beliefs. Self-examination is a choice. Change your idea of who you are and how the world should be, and your perception changes with it. We change our beliefs when we see things from different perspectives. As you challenge the old views that significantly have influence your life and let go of the would's, could's, and should's that you have carried in your thoughts for years, you will no longer experience regret or any other undesired feeling.

More importantly, as you let go of the ideas you have of who you should be or how life should be and **stop resisting life**

as it currently is, you will become free; this is because the fundamental principle of **free will is choosing how you will perceive and react to your experience** in every moment. Nothing we experience eradicates our free will to decide how to respond.

YOU choose how to interpret and react to each one of your life experiences, and this is entirely based on who you believe you are or how you think things should be. If you want to experience a different feeling, then it is as simple as accepting things as they are, step out of the zone of what you "know" and change your beliefs about how a situation or circumstance should be. To step out of your zone of what you "know," you must step away from your concept of what it is, or you won't see it. Being aware allows you to be an observer of your point of view and separate yourself from your current point of view. Practicing awareness will enable you to become the witness to your reactions and the stories that arise from those reactions.

Simply said, to change the circumstances of your life and the world you live in, you must first change your mind. To change your mind, you must change the beliefs that guide your thoughts and emotions. You may implement this change by *paying attention to what you keep saying to yourself and others about yourself and the world*. For instance, when you speak about yourself, what do you say most often? How do you introduce yourself? What do you say to others about money, people, love, relationships, or work? Furthermore, become aware of what's in your life that you often identify with, what you defend, what you are attached to, and what frightens you when you consider giving it up. All of this will give you hints of what you truly believe.

Also, **anxiety and any other negative emotions**, are a sign that a limiting belief is coming up to the surface. Experiencing these emotions provide the perfect opportunity for you to slow down, pay attention, and notice what are you telling yourself about the current situation, How does your body feel: tight, cold, hot, tense? Has your face expression changed? What is the quality of your breathing, shallow, slowly, fast? Ask yourself, am I a hundred percent sure without a doubt that what I'm saying to myself is true?

Another critical way to step out of the "known" zone is by **letting go of the need to know**, the need to understand why things are the way they are. And give up your expectations about how everything is supposed to be. Let go of the obsession with filling in the blanks. Allow your experience to unfold in front of you naturally, without trying to change or make things happen the way you think they "should" be. Likewise, become skeptical and stop accepting everything you believe as true.

Equally important is **giving up the need to be right**. Giving up the need to be right dissolves the need for the Ego to gather evidence or invest lots of effort into constructing your version of what is true to justify your beliefs.

Lastly, a critical step in awareness is **quieting down your mind**. That is why mindfulness meditation is such a crucial tool for changing your beliefs. Long term mindfulness meditation practice allows us to notice our emotional reactions when they happen rather than unconsciously letting them dominate our attention.

Once you do the work to change your thought patterns, your life will change to match your new beliefs. It only requires your awareness and acceptance of what is in this moment. When we're fully present and accept and focus on how things currently are, we feel connected to life and everything in it. This high-vibration feeling attracts positive vibration events into our lives. When your life becomes dictated by thoughts and emotions attached to past events and potential future outcomes, you attract more of what will be, what could be, or what might be. What you focus on, even if you want to or not, creates the energy to bring it into reality.

Your desire to experience a more tolerable state of mind, combined with your beliefs of how to achieve that state of mind, will always be the driver of your choices that can make you run away from what is. However, at the end of the day, the root of the perception of the unfulfilling situation has not been addressed. This pattern will continue repeating until the desire for a peaceful state of mind is so great that you will take steps to change your belief and not the situation. The shift to a new belief immediately begins to create a new experience.

Any feelings that are attached to a thought pattern will resurface each time the pattern is contemplated. Therefore, for you to know life in a new way, counteract and eventually eliminate an unconscious, unproductive thought pattern and associated feelings. You must be willing to begin to pay attention to what you are thinking, moment by moment. To do this, you must look at your dominant thoughts, recognize the cause of disconnect, and embrace the truth and perfection that the situation is offering you, without trying to change it. Staying in balance means always accepting a purpose for what is happening around you.

Remember to not rationalize your actions and feelings based on what you think is coming from intuition; you really do not know if they are coming from intuition—no one knows! It is impossible to know because we have so many memories, thoughts, and beliefs in our subconscious, and our subconscious works too fast for our conscious mind to tell the difference.

Do not get me wrong—I'm not suggesting that intuition does not exist or is not important. What I am suggesting, however, is for you to take a moment to observe and assess if your gut feeling is coming from intuition or from your subconscious. Gut feelings often have a strong emotional component— for example, you may experience a strong attraction or repulsion to a person or place. However, emotional triggers from memories (beliefs) also have a strong emotional feeling, and they feel as if they are real. Take the time to assess if this emotion is really intuition or a feeling generated by a belief.

For most of us there is a lot of gunk in the form of limiting beliefs between us and spirit. We need to focus on clearing this garbage as much as possible. Before assuming a feeling is coming from intuition and acting on a big decision, take the necessary time to process and integrate your feelings and clear any limiting beliefs associated with them. It is not until then that you will know if the message is coming from intuition.

Dr. Hew Len, a renowned teacher of the energy clearing system *Ho'oponopono,* has been known to say he uses *Ho'oponopono* clearing three times before making a decision. If the answer is the same after those clearings, he acts on it. Dr. Len says, "This means if I get an impulse to do something to resolve the perceived problem, I might clean on it three times before

I actually take any action. This is a way to insure the action is coming from inspiration and not memory." This is interesting, since he has been working and dedicating his life to clearing limiting beliefs for over thirty-five years; yet he still clears beliefs daily.

Know that the more you clear limiting beliefs, the more your intuition will become clearer, and the easier it will be to receive inspiration from spirit. Also, become more aware of how your thoughts, feelings, and words create frequencies of energy that you channel into reality. Continually ask questions, be open to embracing new information, challenge long-held ideas and beliefs, and introduce a steady stream of new thoughts that are positive, supportive, and productive, and this will lead you to new choices and actions.

Remember, there is no such thing as "out there." You have created it all. Therefore, if you want to improve your life, you must give yourself a reason to change what you believe in the past and replace it with something new that is true for you. Beliefs can be changed in a moment, but it is not enough to want to change, hope, think, or wish a belief away. The key is to feel as the new belief is real; we must believe it at the core of our being—what Neville Goddard calls "walking in the state of the wish fulfilled."

To feel as our new belief is real sometimes is as simple as finding a logical reason as to why your current belief is not working for you. However, the fact that you have a problem is reason enough to validate that the belief is not working for you. Replace the belief with a new belief that will support the reality that you want to create. One way to validate your new belief is by looking around you and seeing how others have been able to develop the circumstance you wish for—if they can do it, so can you.

The question that often comes up is, "How do I feel something I never experienced before?" For example, let say you have never been married, and your current desire is to be married. It will be difficult for you to imagine the feeling of being married, right? That is because the real question should be, "Why do you want to be married?" One possible answer is to feel companionship, love, and support. This answer tells us more about the belief behind the feeling of what you want to experience. In other words, you believe married people have love, support, and companionship. Now that you know the belief, instead of focusing on the feeling of being married, you can focus on feeling companionship, love, and support. If you have an issue imagining that, then ask yourself, "In how many ways do I currently experience support, love, and companionship in my life?" Once you remember those times, you will have a reference point of the feeling you want to focus on to create the circumstances you desire.

Developing awareness and a new point of view will take patience, persistence, and perseverance. It is a never-ending process. When you think you got it, another belief reveals itself. However, it is worth the work. Awareness of what you believe brings about a fresh start for you to create new beliefs that support a life you love.

PART 3

How It Works:
How Do Your Beliefs
Create Your Reality

Everything is energy and that's all there is to it.
Match the frequency of the reality you want, and
you cannot help but get that reality. It can be no
other way. This is not philosophy. This is physics.
— Albert Einstein

CHAPTER 7

The Energetic Systems of Our Bodies

Our subtle-energy bodies play a major role in maintaining our health. Energy disturbances in the etheric body precede the manifestation of abnormal patterns of cellular organization and growth.
— Richard Gerber

To understand how our beliefs create our experiences and the circumstances of our lives, it is necessary for you to know how our energetic body, also known as energetic anatomy, works. For thousands of years, many different cultures have developed very similar systems that describe what human energy anatomy looks like, how it flows and functions as well as how it interacts with our physical bodies. And from these concepts, many healing and spiritual development systems have been derived.

This section is a brief overview of the elements that compose our energetic anatomy. These energy systems are very complex. *The information that I will provide here is fundamental.*

I will describe the energy systems with enough detail to provide a foundation for you to understand the concepts in this book. Additionally, there are components of our energy anatomy, such as the nadis, hara line, kundalini, and higher dimensional chakras, amongst others, that I won't cover because they do not relate much to the topics covered in this book. If you are interested in learning these systems in detail, many books and articles are dedicated to this concept. I will list a few in Appendix A for your reference.

What I describe in this chapter is based on Eastern philosophy, mainly Chinese, Japanese, and Ayurvedic philosophy, and traditional medicine. According to these traditions, **the energy anatomy of your physical body is composed of your emotions, thoughts, and feelings**. This subtle energy is what carries the information that creates and organizes both your physical and energetic body. It designs your physical structure, health, actions, thoughts, and circumstances.

One way to change your physical body or the circumstances in your life is to shift directly the energy pattern or configuration of your energetic anatomy. This can be done by working directly with your energetic makeup, and using energy medicine techniques, which in turn will automatically create new beliefs to support the new arrangement. Another way to correct imbalances is by starting at the top and changing the beliefs that generated the emotions and feelings that created your current energetic configuration.

It is important to note that if you balance your energy composition without changing or accepting the belief that aligns with the new energy configuration—in other words, if you are stuck in old ways of thinking—sooner or later your energetic structures will revert to their original state, and your body will get sick again or the past circumstances will arise again.

Your energetic body is composed of the following energetic structures or organs.

The Aura

The aura has long been described as an electromagnetic energy field that surrounds people, animals, plants, and objects. The human aura is like a luminous egg-shaped ball of energy that encompasses the body and radiates an emanation that is wider at the bottom than the top. It is believed that the emission is about three feet out from the body. However, the quality and size of this field adjust according to the function being performed and our emotions. Therefore, in some people this field can be larger.

The aura forms your entire consciousness and awareness that guides your life. It is magnetic in nature and attracts experiences toward you. The aura was developed in part by your past life experiences and holds the ideal energetic template to create your current life and attract the necessary circumstances for your spiritual development.

The energetic blueprint of your aura changes during your life, as you grow and develop and new beliefs are formed. The results of your choices, thoughts, emotions, and ideas are reflected in your aura through the type of flow, quality, color, density, and geometric patterns seen in it, and they also become the magnetic forces that attract people, circumstances, and events into your life.

The aura consists of seven levels/layers/auric bodies. Each one of these subtle bodies exists around the physical body and has a specific function or role. They are separate bodies, yet they are all interrelated, and each body affects the others. Each one also has a particular frequency rendered as a different color. The first body is the closest to our physical body, and the seventh is the farthest away. The farther away the layer is from the physical body, the higher its frequency. The size of the layer will be unique to each person, and it directly correlates to how much it has been developed. However, each layer is equally important to the evolution of consciousness and each person.

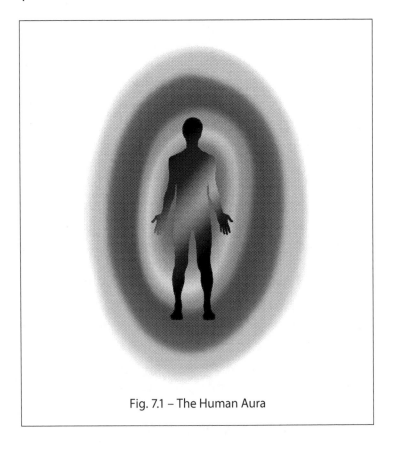

Fig. 7.1 – The Human Aura

The condition of the aura affects a person's feelings, emotions, thought patterns, behavior, and overall health, and vice versa, the state of the physical body impacts the state of the aura. Clearing your aura helps release low-level vibrations and allows you to be aware of your current beliefs and issues and releases them, so you can grow and move beyond your current limitations.

Here is a brief description of each auric body/layer, its function, and how it interacts with our physical body.

- **Level 1: The Etheric or Physical Body**. This layer is the closest to our physical body. It extends about two inches from our physical body, but it also extends internally, surrounding your organs and cells. The color can vary from light to deep blue. People who are holding onto negative emotions or who are dwelling in negativity will have a darker color. This level is highly active, and it changes with every thought, memory, and feeling. For this layer to be in balance, we need physical comfort, pleasure, and health. It also contains the memories of past pain, traumas, health, and pleasure. Additionally, it holds the ideal blueprint for the health of your body in this life. Therefore, blockages in this layer reflect as illnesses in our physical bodies. Working with healing energies at this level triggers a change in the physical body, removes emotional patterns of dysfunction and restores the body back to health.

- **Level 2: The Emotional Body.** This body extends about three inches from our physical body, and it stores our emotional history and experiences. It holds the emotional template for your constitution. This template was created based on your previous lives, and it wires you to feel experiences in a certain way. When this layer is out of balance, you feel sensitive, unstable, and often irrational. This layer is fluid and responds to changes in your emotional states. The color, density, and movement of this body reflect the emotions experienced. The denser, darker colors reflect emotional immaturity or trauma. Lighter colors and frequencies reflect positive emotions. The actual color will be different, depending on the emotion that is being reflected.

- **Level 3: The Mental Body.** This is where our beliefs, values, ideas, intentions, and thought patterns are stored, and they are seen as geometrical patterns. The color is typically seen as bright yellow, and it extends about eight inches from our physical body. The interplay between this layer and your physical layer attracts circumstances, people, and events into your life. Thoughts that are accompanied by strong emotions tend to be exponentially stronger and have more magnetism to attract these life events.

- **Level 4: The Astral/Bridge Body.** This is eight to twelve inches away from the physical body, and it is multicolored. It is the transitional layer of the aura, where the first three layers of the aura reflect our physical nature and presence; the last four layers are the window to our spiritual nature. This body generates the frequencies of sense of love, well-being, expansion, and life-balance, since without love, spiritual frequencies cannot be grounded.

- **Level 5: The Etheric Template Body.** This is one to two feet away from the physical body. This layer holds the ideal blueprint for health and function of a human. In other words, it is the perfect human potential and serves as a carbon copy of the physical body on the spiritual plane. Therefore, if you channel energy from this body to the first layer, you can promote patterns of healing.

- **Level 6: The Celestial Light Body.** This extends two to three feet away from the body and has a shimmering, iridescent quality and color. It reflects our subconscious mind, and it is the seat of spiritual knowledge. This is where the physical mind connects with the spiritual mind. The Celestial body stores our experiences of having a connection to something greater than ourselves.

- **Level 7: The Ketheric or Casual Body.** This body extends about three to five feet from the physical body, and it is composed of a gold-silver color. It protects and holds all other aura layers together, and it contains the blueprint of our spiritual path, reflecting all of the soul's experiences and events through time. This is our link to "Source" or "All That Is," and it receives frequencies from the highest spiritual planes.

All matter inanimate or animate has an aura or energy field. Animate fields are stronger and more easily felt, but both can be used to strengthen your aura. In general, the weaker the auric field, the more susceptible it is to outside influences.

Nature is cleansing and balancing to your aura. Plants, flowers, and trees have dynamic energy fields, and each one has its unique frequency, just like a human does. Because of this, different plants, flowers, or trees can be touched, hugged, or have around you for different effects (see flower essence section on chapter 12). Crystals and stones have electromagnetic properties and the energy released by them as also easily absorb by the auric field. Animals as well have auras than can affect the energy field of your aura.

Due to the electromagnetic nature of the aura, every aura will leave an imprint upon what it interacts with. This interaction can be with a person, the environment, or an object. For instance, if you typically sit in a specific chair or you spend a lot of time in a room, you leave traces, you leave traces of your energy around it. The longer a person has contact with an object, the stronger it becomes charged with an energy pattern that is similar to that of the person.

Also, the longer and the more intimate the contact, the stronger the imprint will be. The more you are exposed to specific energies, the more you are influenced by them, and the more they are influenced by you. If the energy of the other is stronger, it can quickly bring you into resonance with it, the other way around.

Intimate contact such as sexual activity intricately entwines the auric energies and creates a powerful and intimate exchange between those involved. This energy connection and debris can last longer than those that happen through casual contact, and they are not as easily or quickly cleansed or balanced, and the longer the untangling will take. Consequently, you will share this energy with other people you share intimate close experiences and have sex with. This intricate entwinement of energies means there is no such thing as casual sex.

The more prolonged and more intimate the contact with another, the more powerful and subtle the auric interaction is. In close relationships such as close friends, romantic relationships, pets, and family, there is a dynamic entwining and sharing of these energies. For instance, parents, especially the mother, share part of their auric energies with their children throughout their lives.

The Chakras

The chakras are vortices of swirling energy. You could think of the shape of the chakra as a wheel, whirlpool, or funnel. The energy of each chakra can spin either clockwise or counterclockwise. There are hundreds of chakras in the body. However, seven of them—called the primary chakras—are considered the basis of human existence and are associated with each one of the layers of the aura.

"The chakras are specialized energy centers which connect us to the multidimensional universe. The chakras are dimensional portals within the subtle bodies which take in and process energy of higher vibrational nature so that it may be properly assimilated and used to transform the physical body." Says Richard Gerber.

The chakras originate in the hara line, a vertical column to which our chakra attach at their center. Each chakra exchanges energy/information with the aura. They assimilate information coming from the aura and translate it so the body can process it; in addition, any energetic changes in your body and mind are sent to the aura through the chakras. Each of the major chakras is associated with an endocrine gland and conveys emotional and physiological aspects to it.

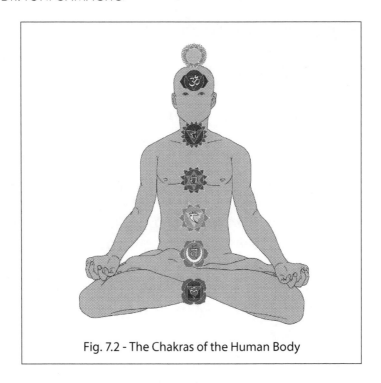

Fig. 7.2 - The Chakras of the Human Body

Here is a little information on each of the chakras and how they interact with the aura.

- **First Chakra – The Root (Muladhara).** It is located at the base of the spine/tail bone area, and it is associated with the adrenal glands. It *processes information from the etheric level of the aura* and supports the vitality of the physical body. This chakra is associated with security and survival issues. Its color is red. The symptoms related to a blockage or weak root chakra are lower back pain, diarrhea, fear, exhaustion, lack of power to confront problems, financial issues, addiction, and lethargy.

- **Second Chakra – Sacral (Svadhisthana).** It is located in the lower abdomen above the pubic bone and beneath the navel area. The second chakra *processes information from the emotional body of the aura,* and it is associated with the reproductive glands. This chakra is related to creative energy, pleasure, overall well-being, and abundance. Its color is orange. When you have a weak or blocked second chakra, you can experience jealousy, lack of sexual desire, urinary tract infections, kidney stones, creative blocks, and poor emotional boundaries; you may also mistake other's emotions for your own. On the other hand, when the chakra is open and balanced, you will have healthy sexual relationships, strong and stable relationships, and a creative life.

• **Third Chakra – Solar Plexus (Manipura).** It is located in the upper abdomen in the stomach area. It *processes information from the mental body of the aura* and is associated with the *pancreas and adrenal glands.* It relates to issues of self-worth, self-esteem, and self-confidence. Its color is yellow. If the chakra is balanced, you will be able to quickly manifest your dreams into reality, and you will be able to understand complex issues. Symptoms when it is out of balance or blocked include stomach ailments, fear, ulcers, bulimia, obesity, indigestion, feelings of victimization, trying to control others, and having a hard time making decisions.

• **The Fourth Chakra – Heart (Anahata).** It is located at the center of the chest, above the heart, and it is associated with the *thymus gland and cardiac plexus.* Its color is green, and it *processes information from the astral body of the aura.* It relates to the ability to give and receive love. Love is the connection between mind, body, and soul and connects everything together. Symptoms when it is out of balance or blocked include heart problems, intolerance, a week immune system, asthma, angina, and lack of joy in life. This chakra deals with issues of self-love, forgiveness, self-validation, self-worth, compassion, and harmony in relationships.

- **The Fifth Chakra – Throat (Vishuda).** It is located in the base of the throat and neck (Adam's apple area). It is associated with the thyroid and parathyroid gland. Its color is blue, and it *processes information from the etheric template body of the aura.* This chakra relates to communication, decision-making, creativity, and truth. It works in conjunction with the second chakra, and when these two are in balance, anything you want can be accomplished. When blocked or out of balance, one may experience a sore throat, dishonesty, thyroid problems, constant talking, shyness, or the inability to speak one's truth to another.

- **The Sixth Chakra – Third Eye (Anja).** It is located slightly above the eyebrows, in the center of the forehead. It is associated with pituitary and pineal glands, and it *processes information from the celestial body of the aura.* Its color is indigo, and it relates to intuition, intelligence, wisdom, and discernment. When there is a blockage in this chakra or it is out of balance, one may experience migraine headaches, tension headaches, eye problems, feeling spaced out, forgetfulness, being too much in one's head, problems staying focused, or a failure to connect with one's inner wisdom.

- **The Seventh Chakra – Crown (Sahasrara).** It is located at the top of the head. It governs the pituitary and pineal glands, and it *process information from the ketheric body of the aura*. Its color is violet or pure white light. It relates to inspiration, oneness with the universe or God, divinity, present moment awareness, and inner wisdom. When is blocked or out of balance, one may experience confusion, dominance, lack of self-awareness, mental illness, worry, dizziness, or looking outside yourself for answers.

By unblocking the chakras, your energy pathways will clear and balance, and harmony will be restored in your physical and energetic bodies.

The Meridians

The meridians are channels in the body that have no material form and transmit subtle energy as a vital life force named **qi** (pronounced chee). You can look at them as an energy highway of the human body. They are mapped throughout the body and have access to all parts of the body and the chakras. The qi that travels through the meridians is encoded with the necessary information for the body to function at a cellular level.

Qi is a key concept in Chinese medicine, and it is similar to the term *prana* (life force) of India; it is known as *ki* in Japan. Qi is a vital essence found in all things, and it comprises the material and nonmaterial. I will refer primarily to its expression as energy, keeping in mind that energy and matter are changeable into one another.

In its pure form, qi is subtle and refined. It is a substance with no form (energy). On the other hand, matter is a condensed, slowed-down form of qi. *The sources of qi in the body are from food, air, water, emotions, and the essences of the kidneys* (which some part of this qi we are born with), *combined with the energy that has come from the aura* and processed through the chakras.

How well we use qi from these sources will depend on our lifestyle and attitudes. Whatever manifests in our bodies will be an expression of how well we use qi. For example, a graceful person has harmonious qi. Weak people lack qi, strong people have abundant qi, and people with clear minds have refined, as opposed to confused, qi.

Qi that stagnates causes accumulations, resulting in negative emotions, obesity, tumors, cysts, cancers, and viral and yeast-related diseases that usually arise with a sedentary lifestyle, harmful emotions, and a poor diet. Exercise, herbal therapy, yoga, qigong, acupuncture, and awareness practices, such as meditation, are ways that we can clear obstructions and maximize qi.

Traditional Chinese and Japanese medicine recognizes twelve organ meridians and five extraordinary meridians throughout the body where qi or energy flows. Each of the twelve organ channels corresponds to the five yin organs, the six yang organs, and the pericardium and San Jiao. Even though organ meridians have the same names of the organs in our physical body, they should not be thought of as being identical with the physical anatomical organs of the body.

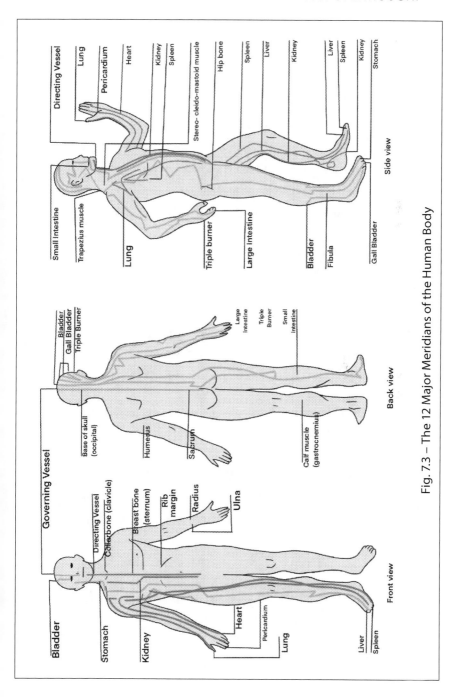

Fig. 7.3 – The 12 Major Meridians of the Human Body

The Five Elements

All energy in the physical plane can be classified into five elements. The elements are wood, fire, earth, metal, and water. They are also known as the five phases or five transformations. The five elements system is a comprehensive template that organizes all natural phenomena into five groups or patterns. It is important to remember that the elements are merely names or symbols used to describe five different types of energies in nature and our bodies. They are not the energy itself.

By categorizing the meridians into the five elements, they show us how the structures and systems in our bodies are connected to each other, how we are connected to our environment and the natural world, and how our world is part of the greater universe. They are a diagnostic tool that, along with other theories, can help us understand what is currently shaping our life and physical, mental, and spiritual health.

This table outlines the organ meridians classified within the five elements.

Element	Organ Meridian
Wood (air)	liver, gallbladder
Fire	heart, small intestine, pericardium, triple heater
Earth	stomach, pancreas, spleen
Metal	lung, large intestine
Water	kidney, bladder

Each element has a part to play to keep the ecosystem balanced, and they intertwine and balance one another to keep our bodies healthy. Disruption of one of the five element energies increases the risk of emotional disturbances or interruption in the pattern of flow of energy in our bodies. As a result, the disease could progress from one organ to another because of lack of nourishment, overcontrol, or abuse of an elemental energy. This imbalance of energy may also lead a person to experience specific life events, ailments, or emotions.

How the Elements Influence One Another

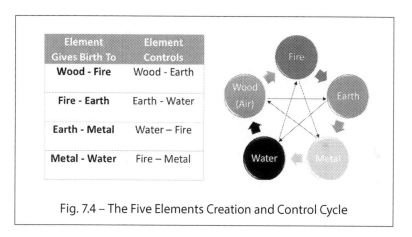

Element Gives Birth To	Element Controls
Wood - Fire	Wood - Earth
Fire - Earth	Earth - Water
Earth - Metal	Water – Fire
Metal - Water	Fire – Metal

Fig. 7.4 – The Five Elements Creation and Control Cycle

- Every element has an element that "creates" it (the mother) and an element that "controls" it.

- The mother "creates" or "feeds" the organ (its son) in the cycle through a strengthening flow of energy. If the element son becomes deficient, it may draw excessively from the preceding element (its mother) and deplete. At the same time, it won't have the ability to strengthen the next element.

- Each element is said to control, check, or regulate another.

- An element can become hyperactive or excessive, and overcontrol or destroy another, causing the controlled element to become deficient.

- An element that should be controlled can become excessive and in turn control the element that normally controls it. This is akin to the child rebelling and insulting or trying to discipline its father.

How to Remember the Cycle

Creation Cycle	Control Cycle
Wood burns to make	Wood is cut by metal
Fire whose ashes decompose	Fire is extinguished by water
Earth which is born and mined	Earth is penetrated by wood
Metals which enrich	Metal is melted by fire
Water which nourishes trees (wood)	Water is channeled and contained by earth

The elements and organs are not solitary, fixed entities but interrelated flows of energies and substances in a state of transformation. Each element includes categories, such as seasons, body tissues, emotions, colors, tastes, and sounds, which show us when that element is in harmony or when it is deficient. (See table 7.1)

All related categories or correspondences to the element **respond to changes to the organ**. For example, if you work on liver, you may be able to see emotional changes in the person, like less anger, improved vision, stronger and more flexible tendons and ligaments, a healthier gallbladder, etc. Conversely, by developing patience and strengthening ligaments and tendons, you may resolve an issue with the liver. (To better understand this example, see "liver" in the "wood" column on table 7.1.)

Each chakra is linked and corresponds primarily to one or more elements. However, to a certain degree, all elements are affected by all of the seven chakras. These are the elemental correspondences of each chakra:

Element	Chakra
Wood	heart
Fire	solar plexus
Earth	root
Metal	throat, third eye and crown
Water	sacral

Table 7.1. Elemental Correspondences/Categories					
	Water	Wood (Air)	Fire	Earth	Metal
Movement	Flowing	Rising	Radiating	Grounding	Gathering
Organs	Kidney Bladder	Liver Gallbladder	Heart Small intestine	Stomach Spleen Pancreas	Lungs Large intestine
Personality traits	openness, courage, flow	direction, freshness, spontaneity	excitement, variety	nurturing, safety, compassion	dependability, regularity
Natural skill	flexibility, adaptability	creating new activity	expansion, inspiration	focus, carry through	completing, moving on
Natural challenge	integrating change, flow	loss of freedom	focusing on one endeavor	being alone	completing moving on
Emotion out of balance (unhealthy)	fear, insecurity, backing away	anger when controlled, frustration, impatience, rage	excitement, laughing, scattered, manic ups and downs, joy	pity, suspicion, gossip, victim, blames others, abandoned, worry, anxiety	sadness, guilt, depression, blame self, controlling, inferiority, shame, grief, melancholy

Table 7.1. Elemental Correspondences/Categories	Water	Wood (Air)	Fire	Earth	Metal
Emotion in balance (healthy)	adventurous, adaptable, go with the flow	spontaneity, organization, patience, fresh	radiant, inspiring, charismatic	empathetic, supporting	dependable, successful, complete
Relationship strength	seeing overall, big view, intuitive, awareness	discovering, empowering, new direction	inspiring, passionate	bonding, listening	commitment, devotion
Relationship weakness	easily detached	power quest	multiple interests	insecure, blaming others	guilt, shame, being right or wrong
Tone of voice	apologetic, groaning, timid	directing, shouting	excited, verbose	singing, whine	monotone, choked
Emotive response	shivers	Gripping	hyperactive, nervous	sobbing, energy draining	stuck, isolated, barren
Season	winter	Spring	summer	early fall	autumn
Body association	bones, head, hair	muscle, tendons, ligaments, nails	blood vessels, face color, complexion	interstitial fluid, lymph, breast, upper lip	skin, breath, body hair
Body fluids	urine	Tears	perspiration	saliva	mucus, snivel

Table 7.1. Elemental Correspondences/Categories					
	Water	Wood (Air)	Fire	Earth	Metal
Sense organ	hearing	Vision	taste	touch	smell
Environment	cold	Wind	heat	moisture	dryness
Imbalanced order	putrefying (e.g., urine)	oily, greasy (e.g., rancid oil)	burning, scorched (e.g., burned toast)	stale sweetness (e.g., old perfume)	rancid (e.g., fecal matter)
Complexion hue	grayish	dark brown, yellow, green	red	orange, yellow	sallow, pale white
Harmonizing color	dark shades, soothing rustic, blue, purple, black	bright, fresh, pure, green	inspiring yet grounding colors	yellow, orange	white
Harmonizing recommendations	small challenges	free play and recreation, avoid pressure (e.g., competition)	focus, one step at a time	supportive environment, accept role as a participant	variety, forgive
Harmonizing taste	salty	Sour	bitter	sweet	pungent
Harmonizing grains	buckwheat, beans	barley, wheat, rye	corn, amaranth, quinoa	millet	brown rice

Table 7.1. Elemental Correspondences/Categories					
	Water	Wood (Air)	Fire	Earth	Metal
Harmonizing vegetables	seaweeds (cooked), beans	rising greens (e.g., leeks, onions, celery, sprouts)	large leafy greens (e.g., kale, collards, dandelion)	round vegetables (e.g., squash, pumpkin, cabbage, cauliflower)	contracted plants, roots (e.g., radish, onion, burdock, carrot)
Harmonizing fruits	winter and dried fruits	spring fruits	summer fruits	late summer fruits	autumn fruits

Energy Flow Between the Components
of Our Energetic Anatomy

As stated in chapters 1, you interact with different dimensions and realities through your energetic anatomy. These dimensions and realities have a frequency that is broadcasted as vibrations of energy. The aura functions like an antenna that receives these frequencies and then filters and passes them to the chakras. Frequency coming down the aura needs to be transformed into a level (frequency) that the physical body can handle, without overloading the nervous system. This is where the chakras come in; they translate this information into lower levels that the body can assimilate and through the meridians make it available to your physical body and mind. The meridians provide energy to every cell in your body, and the nervous system uses this information to integrate with your level of awareness.

Often the energy components of our energetic anatomy are looked at separately. There are countless books and websites out there dedicated to each separate part. For example, books may be dedicated only to chakras, giving us the impression that they are an independent organ of energy with its own functions and that they can be treated as such; however, the energy components are all interconnected. They interact and affect each other as well as occupy the same space. If one component changes, it affects and changes the rest. The only thing that differentiates one from the other is their different frequency.

The transmission of energy through these systems is bidirectional. Energy flowing through the meridians gathers information from your cells and then is transferred back to the chakras. In addition to this information, the chakras collect information from your thoughts and emotions, and everything is sent to the aura, where it gets radiated outward, relaying the quality and vibration of your being. This frequency is what attracts the reality you are experiencing, by drawing the reality that matches your vibration and attracting the people and situations in your life that match that vibration. In other words, your aura picks up only the frequencies that it is compatible with. So as you change your beliefs, the energy of your aura changes and you create a new reality.

Therefore, a disruption or block in any of these systems can manifest in poor health, adverse circumstances, or negative emotions. These blocks or disturbances can be created by poor quality food, stress, beliefs that no longer serve us, and environmental toxins. Remember that the communication between these systems is bidirectional, and the meridians touch every cell in our body. If the quality of the cell is weak, the frequency of the energy passed to the aura will be low vibration, consequently attracting undesirable circumstances into your life.

CHAPTER 8

Your Electric Body

Fear, by its depressing effect on our mentality, thus
causes disharmony in our physical and magnetic
bodies and paves the way for [bacterial] invasion. The
real cause of disease lies in our own personality...
— Richard Gerber

Eastern philosophy explains that everything in the universe is composed of two complementary opposite energies (yin and yang) that flow between heaven and earth. The Chinese character "yin" means the shadow side of a mountain, "yang" the sunny side of a mountain. Yin and yang's energies are contrary but perfectly complementary.

Yang refers to the energy of the cosmos spiraling centripetally towards the earth. The properties of yang energy are more downward, dense, inward, physical, material. Yin is the energy of the earth that spirals towards the cosmos in an opposite, centrifugal direction. Yin is an expanding force, and its properties are more upwards, light, mental, outward, psychological, and spiritual in orientation.

The following table outline some of the general aspects of yin and yang.

Yin	Yang
Feminine	Masculine
Earth	Sun
Softer	Hard
Moon	Heaven
Dark	Light
Receptivity	Resistance
Passivity	Activity
Body structure	Body Function
Rest	Active
Night	Day
West	East
Material	Energy
Produces form	Immaterial
Energy consolidation (in macrobiotics is the opposite)	Energy expansion (opposite in macrobiotics)
Descending energy	Ascending energy
Water	Fire
Front of the body	Back and Left (and left side of the body too)
Dark side of the mountain	Sunny side of the mountain
Negative	Positive
Moisture	Dryness
Slowness	Restless

Everything in the universe, including our body, is composed of these two forces, and nothing is only Yin or Yang. Yin and yang properties are always in dynamic equilibrium. As one aspect declines, the other increases to an equal degree. For instance, after day (yang) follows night (yin), after rest (yin) activity occurs (yang). If the balance of yin and yang are missing, Qi (life force or energy) is blocked. This blockage can cause physical or emotional discomfort and can lead to illness.

Yin and yang energy is further differentiated into the system of the five elements discussed in chapter 7 to gain a deeper understanding of the body, mind, and spirit. These phases represent the seasons of the earth, named as wood, fire, earth, metal, and water. These elements also match with the stages of human life: birth, growth, maturation, death, and rebirth. The movement through these phases is reflected in both the external environment and the human internal environment. This cycle is represented at every level of life - from the rotation of the planets to the function of internal organs.

In the same way, as our life force (qi) is flowing through our bodies, it seems that all living beings also radiate natural electromagnetic energy. Dr. Robert Becker's work demonstrated this electromagnetic energy. In his work, Dr. Becker showed that living organisms and animals show a direct current of electric charge, which is measurable from their body surface. He concluded that the weak electrical currents that flow through our bodies have much to do with healing and regeneration of cells [27].

Becker studied regeneration after lesions such as limb amputation in salamanders and frogs. He hypothesized that electric fields played an essential role in controlling the regeneration process. Becker demonstrated this by mapping the electric potentials at different body parts during the regeneration, showing that the central part of the body commonly was positive, and the limbs were negative. For instance, when a limb of a salamander or a frog was amputated, the voltage at the cut (measured near to the central part of the body) changed from about -10 mV (millivolts) to +20 mV or more the next day—a phenomenon called the current of injury.

In a frog, the voltage would go back to the typical negative level in four weeks or so, and no limb regeneration would take place. However, in a salamander (an animal that usually regenerates limbs after amputation), the voltage during the first two weeks would change from the +20 mV to -30 mV, and then normalize (to -10 mV) during the next two weeks—and the limb would be regenerated [27].

Becker discovered a connection between the current of injury and regeneration. Many years and experiments later, he and his colleagues using electrical current have grown back a frog's leg from elbow to toes and a rat's leg from shoulder to the top half of the elbow, with cartilage and bone, muscle, nerves and veins, all in impressive anatomical precision. And now reached the point where they can confidently predict that regeneration of human parts can and will be achieved [28].

Further, Dr. Becker, as Nikola Tesla, believed that if you could eliminate specific outside frequencies that interfered in our bodies, we would have higher resistance toward disease. In fact, Dr. Becker was one of the first people to lead the opposition to high-voltage power lines. And he has been named as one of the most influential figures in the area of anti-EMF activism.

Additionally, in the early 1920s Royal Raymond Rife, M.D. found that with specific frequencies (Mortal Oscillatory Rate), he could destroy a cancer cell. As well as certain microorganisms, including bacteria, viruses, and parasites [29]. He also discovered that specific frequencies could prevent the development of a disease, and others would destroy disease by chattering the pathogen. In much the same way opera singers match the frequencies of wine glasses with their voice and shatter them.

On this basis in 1934, he conducted medical trials with incredible results. In one of his studies with 16 terminally ill patients with various cancers, the committee declared the first 14 patients cured of their disease within 70 days after exposing the patients to specific frequencies. The remaining two were said cured three weeks later. Amazingly, the patients only required two 3-minute sessions per week to achieve total recovery. Rife found that more-frequent courses didn't allow the lymphatic system enough time to take up the released toxins from the destroyed microorganism or cancer and remove them from the body. [30]

Also, Bjorn Nordenstrom, a radiologist of Stockholm, Sweden, found in the 1980s that the human body has electropositive and electronegative energy fields. He discovered that by putting an electrode inside a tumor and running a milliamp D.C. current through the electrode, he could destroy the cancer tumor and stop its growth. [31]

Furthermore, Bruce Tainio, of Tainio Technology and head of the Department of Agriculture at Eastern Washington

University, developed a Calibrated Frequency Monitor (CFM) that was used to measure the human frequency. Tainio measured a person's frequency by taking readings on various points of the body and averaging them. He concluded that the higher the rate in the body, the better the health. And he estimated that the healthy body has a frequency between 62 and 72 MHz, and disease starts when the frequency drops below this range. Other of his findings are:

- Cells in our body can begin to change (mutate) when the rate drops below 62MHz.

- 58 MHz is the frequency of the body when you are sick with the cold or the flu.

- When candida is present, the body vibrates at a rate of 55MHz.

- In a body with Epstein-Barr virus present, frequencies have been measured as 52 MHz.

- At a frequency of 42 MHz, cancer can appear in the body.

- The frequency of the body has been measured at 20 MHz when the death process begins.

Substances with low vibration, lower your own frequency just by being in your energy field. Therefore, every choice you make daily, no matter how small, is affecting the quality of your frequency. These choices include the thoughts you think, the food you eat, how you react to stress, what you watch on tv, and your feelings. All these raise or lower your vibration — even the people you spend time with impact your heart and brain waves.

It is a known fact that a substance or person with a higher frequency can cause the vibration of a substance or person with a lower frequency to increase. Therefore, being in the presence of high-vibrating people raises your vibration!

In their studies, the Institute of HeartMath and others have demonstrated this change in heart and brain waves when someone touches a person or is even a few feet away from a person and is emitting vibrations that carry emotions such as gratitude, lust, anger, compassion or shame [30]. The concluded that experiencing negative emotions can create a nervous system and heart chaos and that not only impact our health but the health of those around our electromagnetic field. "We are fundamentally and deeply connected with each other and the planet itself, and what we do individually really does count and matters," states Rolin McCratey, PhD, director of research at the HeartMath Institute.

The frequency of your entire being is what dictates your physical and emotional health. This vibration turns into qi, which moves through the meridians, up the chakras, until it reaches your aura. Where it attracts the reality that matches your vibration, therefore, raising your physical vibration is the key to achieving the life you may be dreaming of. Moreover, when you continuously are vibrating at a high frequency, you will feel fantastic, electrically charged, and alive. You will also attract high-quality opportunities, people, and favorable circumstances in your life.

We can raise the frequency of our bodies to a healthy level in many ways. From yoga, mudras, meditation, sound therapy, and all the other energy medicine modalities covered part seven of this book. However, you can live a high-frequency life by merely choosing from the high vibration's options of the tasks and actions you must engage daily. For instance, you have to eat every day, therefore to raise your vibration, you can choose to eat only high-frequency foods.

Your vibration is impacted by everything around you through the principle of entrainment. Entrainment is the inclination for two oscillating bodies to lock into phase so that they vibrate in harmony. Since everything has a frequency, you can raise your vibration quickly by associating yourself with or ingesting higher vibration items. Also minimizing your exposure to low vibration things you can prevent your vibration from lowering.

As you can see, you can raise your vibration in many ways — however, one of the most important and critical ways by nourishing ourselves with **high-frequency foods**. Not only are you what you think, but you are also what you eat. Therefore, to increase your frequency, make sure you are consuming foods that have a high vibration and avoid foods that lower your frequency.

The most high-vibration foods are plant-based and in season. Notably, food that is alive, fresh, organic and is grown with clean and sustainable farming practices by people who care has the highest frequency, such as living greens like kale, broccoli, wheatgrass, herbs, raw nuts. Followed by slightly cook foods like cooked vegetables, whole grains, and legumes. Dead food like animal protein has been found to have the lowest frequency. Unfortunately, canned, and the rest of the processed foods, such as fast food, showed a frequency of cero!

The chemistry and frequencies of fresh foods (including herbs) can help humans maintain the optimal frequency to the degree that disease cannot exist. It best to avoid processed food entirely and to make sure you are eating more fresh food such as vegetables, grains, and fruits. That alone is going to increase your frequency.

If you eat meat or any other animal protein, ensure that it is organic and free-range. Eating animals raised on unhealthy food and treated with hormones, antibiotics, and synthetic growth promoters add to our level of toxicity. Additionally, long-term consumption of animal protein above the current recommended dietary allowance for adults (RDA: 0.8 g protein/ kg body weight/day) has been linked with osteoporosis, kidney disease, calcium stones in the urinary tract, and some cancers.

Moreover, it is a known fact that non-organic animals are raised in inhumane ways. Are also stressed, suffer, and in the case of cattle are feed grains instead of grass. Therefore, their vibration is low. The energy of an animal is the highest when it is healthiest, and this happens when it is raised in its natural habitat, and it feeds what is natural to them. Organic animals meet these criteria. Particularly cattle, they are raised on pasture, their outdoor access cannot be restricted, and they are free to engage in natural behaviors. Any shelters provided for the animals ensures their comfort and still allow the opportunity for exercise and movement. Organic animals are raised in a stress-free and humane manner. Therefore, their vibration is higher.

Also, avoid other foods that lower your frequency, such as coffee (caffeine), alcohol, and other drugs. As depressant alcohol and marijuana slow down your metabolic system and make I harder for you to raise your vibration. Similarly, even though caffeine can provide a temporary high when its effects wore down you crash, lowering your vibration.

Artificial sweeteners, pesticides, MSG, hydrogenated oils, and any other synthetic or altered food are not only neurotoxins and endocrine disruptors, but they also lower your vibration. Avoid genetically modified/engineered food (GE) as much as possible, GEs may be altering the nonvisible aspects of the plant, like its life essence. Scientists say that GE plants are identical to non-GE. However, they are observing that chemical compounds of GE plants are similar to non-GE, but they can't see if their life essence (energy) is the same [32].

According to Traditional Chinese Medicine, the genetic aspects of an organism function within its life essence. Consequently, a change in its genetic composition (GE) may cause damage to its life essence. Therefore, damage to the life essence of our food produced by GE may not create damage to its nutrients. Instead, it could cause dysfunction in its realm of influence (energetics) in humans, such as our vitality, fertility, immunity, hormonal function, higher awareness, and graceful aging [32].

Do not confuse the vibration of food with its life force (qi). The energetics of foods will be discussed in detail in chapter 12. However, it is worth noting here that Qi (life force or energy) is mainly concentrated in seeds and grains as in the case of brown rice. Beans, nuts, and sea vegetables also retain their vitality over time. Therefore, meals should include plenty of land vegetables to balance the strong life force of the grains, legumes, nuts, and seeds.

Further, the key to health, happiness, and longevity is **preparing balanced, beautiful meals from high quality and whole or traditionally processed foods**. By preparing whole foods, primarily plant-based, we not only raise our vibration, but we also begin to nourish our bodies on a level that promotes cellular regeneration, appreciation for life, and a general sense of well-being.

Last but not least, food is not only energy, but it is also spirit. Therefore, blessing your food also lifts its vibration. Consequently, one of the most important aspects of cooking is to consciously infuse our food with gratitude, love, and other positive energy. Calm, peaceful and family-oriented cooking and community living bring health to the individual, unity, and love to the family, and peace to society. Therefore, take the time to bless each meal for the health of our family, community, and the planet.

Equally crucial to eating a high-frequency and nutrient-dense diet is learning to **discipline your mind**. Negative emotions sustained over time can change our vibrational frequency and manifest in illness and adverse circumstances. After all, there are quite a few studies that show that chronic emotional stress is more predictive of death from cancer and heart disease than cigarette smoking! You are 40 percent more likely to die of one of those diseases if you chronically experience low-vibration emotions than a person that moves past challenges with grace. Likewise, a positive mental attitude, prayer, and meditation can raise our vibration and promote favorable circumstances.

To demonstrate this, Dr. David Hawkins, a nationally renowned psychiatrist, physician, researcher, spiritual teacher, and lecturer created the international known an applied "map of consciousness" [33] which he created based on 20 years of research and clinical study. The "Map of Consciousness" incorporates findings from quantum physics, kinesiology, and nonlinear dynamics.

Hawkins explains that each emotion generates a different frequency, and a person vibrates accordingly to the feelings he experiences most often. He states, people based on their beliefs, tend to experience certain emotions chronically. The frequencies from these emotions can be summed up and averaged to know the person's default frequency level or what he labels their "level of consciousness." While a person usually vibrates at a default – "normal" frequency, someone will rarely maintain the same consciousness level at any one period. They instead shift to a couple of levels higher and lower depending on the circumstances.

Hawkins rates each state of consciousness and emotions on a scale from 20 to 1,000. This is his scale from low to high:

Force			Power		
Level	Rate	Emotion	Emotion	Rate	Emotions
Shame	20	Humiliation	Neutrality	250	Trust
Guilt	30	Blame	Willingness	310	Optimism
Apathy	50	Despair	Acceptance	350	Forgiveness
Grief	75	Regret	Reason	400	Understanding
Fear	100	Anxiety	Love	500	Reverence
Desire	125	Craving	Joy	540	Serenity
Anger	150	Hate	Peace	600	Bliss

| Pride | 175 | Scorn | Enlightenment | 700-1000 | Ineffable |
| Courage | 200 | Affirmation | | | |

Hawkins segmented these emotions into two main categories: one based on what he calls force (<200) and the other based on what he calls power (>200). He states that people in levels of force vibrate in fear-based emotions. They favor exercising control over others or themselves (oppression, force, coercion, manipulation, violence) to achieve their desired outcome — for example, crime, war, abuse, and authoritative leadership and parenting styles. On the other hand, people in levels of power vibrate in love-based emotions. They are in tune with themselves, live in the present moment more often, and respect fundamental human rights.

Chronic anger, depression, anxiety, worry, jealousy, and all the other emotions that fall below 200 on Hawkins' scale are toxic and will keep your vibration low. So, the best thing you can do to move toward a high-vibration life is get serious about processing, reframing, and releasing the negative beliefs that are creating these emotions in you. As explained in chapter 6, being aware of your thoughts and feelings is the key to overcoming a limiting belief.

A technique often used to learn to recognize negative thoughts as they come up so we can become more realistic in our thinking is cognitive restructuring. This technique can help us see an event that is causing us stress more clearly; reduce the tunnel vision that often arises while we are under stress, and minimize false alarms that sometimes show up when we are under stress.

Cognitive restructuring is a potent therapy technique. However, one disadvantage of this technique is that it is sometimes difficult for people to learn without the assistance of a therapist or a coach. This is because the stories we tell ourselves to validate our current set of beliefs are like autosuggestions that hypnotize us and make it hard for us to see that other possibilities exist. Therefore, we often can't identify the perception (belief) that is causing us distress, or we are focused on justifying (reasoning) the way we think. It is also common for people to believe they are doing the technique right, when, in fact, they are not. And incorrectly conclude that the method does not work. Nevertheless, here is one exercise that you can try on your own:

1. The first step is to become aware of negative thoughts. Becoming aware of your thoughts is one of the most challenging parts of the exercise because negative thoughts tend to be automatic. You can do this by monitoring and recording events during the day that caused you to stress. Write them down.

2. At the end of the day or when you have time, review the situation. Think about what thoughts when through your mind during this event. Write them down. Look for distortions or dysfunctional beliefs. Do certain conditions trigger negative thought patterns? Are you a black-and-white thinker in specific topics? Do you typically experience anger or sadness in response to stress?

3. The next step is to reframe the negative thoughts by writing down more accurate, adaptive thoughts about the event. Reframing thoughts is not always easy, but these questions can help you:

a. Are my thoughts on the event correct?

b. Am I 100 percent sure, without a doubt that I'm correct?

c. Am I using words such as *never, always, worst, terrible,* or *horrible* to describe the event?

d. What objective evidence or facts exist to support my view? In other words, what evidence do I have that this situation will turn out this way?

e. Am I overemphasizing a negative aspect of this event or person?

f. What positive alternative views are there for the event?

g. Am I catastrophizing, awfulizing, jumping to conclusions, and assuming an adverse outcome?

h. Is there anything positive about this situation?

i. Am I undervaluing my ability to cope with the event?

j. How much will this matter next week, in a month, or year?

k. If I had one month to live, how important will this be?

l. What is the worst that can happen if my view of the event is correct?

m. What actions can I take to influence the event?

n. What is the worst thing that could happen to my family or me? How does this event compare to that?

4. After thinking things through, restate your original beliefs regarding the event, so they are more realistic and less distorted. You can do this by rewriting your original thought. Write down new positive ways of thinking or more helpful beliefs that direct to a new approach to deal with the event.

With a little practice, you will learn to identify and correct stress-inducing thoughts as they arise. Consequently, you will find yourself feeling less stress and happier. Note that disciplining your mind is not about suppressing, ignoring, stuffing, or faking your emotions. It is about most of the time, not letting negative feelings or adverse events hijack your life for too long or at all.

Therefore, when negative emotions arise, take a few minutes (about 90 seconds) to feel the emotion. Then recognize it as a learning opportunity and shift as soon as you can to a positive feeling. In these times you can change to a positive vibration quickly, by thinking about things that you are grateful for. After all, you cannot feel two different emotions at once. Alternatively, using the Ho'oponopono technique explained in chapter 12 is also a quick and easy way to shift your vibration.

According to Cicero (106–43 BC), gratitude is not only the greatest of the virtues but the parent of all of the others. You will be surprised how the simple act of **gratitude** can change your life for the better. Not only will it improve your health, it will also lift your vibration and bring you into harmony with the energy of the universe, which in turn will attract more good things into your life to be grateful for.

Practicing gratitude also improves emotional and physical Well-being. "Gratitude unlocks the fullness of life. It turns what we have into enough, and more. It turns denial into acceptance, chaos to order, confusion to clarity. It can turn a meal into a feast, a house into a home, a stranger into a friend," said Melody Beattie. "The practice of gratitude can have dramatic and lasting effects in a person's life," commented Robert A. Emmons, a leading scientific expert on the science of gratitude at UC Davis. Gratitude is associated with optimism, and studies have discovered that grateful people are happier, less stressed, and less depressed and receive more social support. Emmons believes gratitude allows individuals to celebrate the present and be an active participant in their own lives. By focusing on valuing and appreciating friends, oneself, situations, and circumstances, it focuses the mind of an individual on what he or she already has rather than something that's missing and is needed.

Gratitude is associated with higher levels of good cholesterol (HDL) and lower levels of bad cholesterol (LDL). People who write in a gratitude journal for fifteen minutes before they go to bed sleep better and longer. [34] Grateful people experience fewer aches and pains, lower blood pressure (even when under stress), and improved mental clarity, and they report feeling healthier than other people do. [35] Robert Emmons has concluded that gratitude improves psychological health such as increasing happiness and reducing depression. It also reduces toxic emotions, such as envy, resentment, frustration, and regret. Additionally, gratitude enhances empathy, reduces aggression, and improves self-esteem.

Gratitude increases mental strength and resilience, reduces stress, and helps to overcome trauma. [36], [37] Practicing gratitude led to a 7 percent reduction in biomarkers of inflammation in patients with congestive heart failure. [38] Keeping a gratitude diary for two weeks produced sustained reductions in perceived stress by 28 percent and depression by 16 percent. [39]

Gratitude lower levels of cortisol (stress hormones) by 23 percent. A daily gratitude practice can decrease the effects of neurodegeneration that occurs with increasing age. Writing a letter of gratitude reduced feelings of hopelessness in 88 percent of suicidal inpatients and increased levels of optimism in 94 percent. Grateful people have between 9 to 13 percent lower levels of Hemoglobin A1c, a key marker of glucose control that plays a vital role in diabetes. [40]

In addition to high-frequency food and emotions, you can *raise your vibration by engaging in deeply meditative and intimate sex*. The act of sexual intercourse is the most intense form of energy exchange there is. Consequently, sex is one of the most potent ways to raise your vibration, and we should honor the power of this exchange. This mingling of energies is most beneficial when we truly know and trust our partner, when we feel safe with them, and when we are resonating on a similar frequency.

However, many people confuse sex and intimacy. For that reason, trivial sexual experiences with chaotic frequencies are prevalent nowadays. Unfortunately, when disturb and disconnected frequencies collide, it can be jarring and damaging to the whole person. Especially for energetically sensitive people, and it can take them an extended period to recover from a low-vibration sexual interaction. On the other hand, intimate loving sex not only does it feel good, but it is also therapeutic and can raise your vibration. So, to raise your vibration with sex, it is essential to reconnect sexual experience to the powerful and positive energetic practice is meant to be. Let me be clear. I'm not stating that casual sex is "wrong" or "bad." I'm only saying that creates low vibration states; on the other hand, intimacy produces high vibrations.

A technique to further increase your vibration with sexual energy is the ancient Buddhist, Hindu, and Taoist practice for conserving and building sexual energy – Tantra, and Taoism. Tantra and Taoist are about connection — whether that's with yourself or between you and a partner. The word Tantra originated from the ancient Sanskrit — means "web" or "to weave energy."

Tantra promised enlightenment in a single lifetime to those who cultivated pleasure, vision, and ecstasy instead of avoiding it [41]. The heart of Tantra and Taoism is the elimination of duality. Therefore, the purpose was to achieve and experience a oneness between sexual partners that might be had between an individual and the rest of creation.

When you practice Tantra or Taoism, you and your partner learn to be physically and spiritually present. You give each other energy that continues to grow even after you've finished having sex. Therefore, creating a deeper, more harmonious bond with your partner that allows you both to explore and expand all aspects of your personalities. So that you can truly know the other person.

This practice is also used to cultivate Qi for ecstasy, vitality, and health. Our body is dependent on qi. By learning to circulate, and store qi, and especially by focusing on the flow of qi from the sexual organs to the rest of the body, the practice of Tantra will not only cultivate more powerful and balanced sexual energy, but will also affect their overall energy, immune function, mental clarity, and spiritual awareness.

Tantra and Taoism are not limited to those with a partner, and you can practice on your own too. Regardless if you're single or with a partner, these techniques will deepen your relationships, enhance your overall vitality, and bring a blissful energy flow into your life.

Lastly, you can **utilize nature to raise your vibration**, counteract the effects of environmental toxins, and heal and prevent chronic illness. A growing body of research is now demonstrating that exposure to nature or its elements can result in beneficial effects such as improved cognition and psychological well-being, lowered blood pressure, reduced stress, and faster healing. In fact, a simple view of nature out of a window can help patients heal faster. For example, in one study with patients recovering from gallbladder surgery, those who had a view of trees recovered more quickly than patients whose windows faced a brick wall. [42]

Furthermore, research shows that **nature also has a positive effect on your immune system**. "Your immune system doesn't only communicate with other organs and systems in your body; it also communicates with the outside world. It is a sensory organ that is made to receive information that you are not able to consciously receive," states Clemens G. Arvay in his book, The Biophilia Effect. [43]

He goes on and states, "One day spent in the wilderness increases the number of our natural killer cells in the blood by 40 percent on average. If you spend two days in a row in a wooded area, you can raise the number of your natural killer cells by more than 50 percent."

What is more impressive is that those who spent just one day in the forest will have more natural killer cells in their bodies for seven days after. Even if they did not go back during that time. Other studies on the effects of nature on our well-being have shown:

- Walking in the forest decreases blood glucose levels of type 2 diabetics. Moreover, merely being present in the forest lowers blood sugar. [42]

- Nature alleviates pain, even if only observed by a window. [42] In fact, significant reduction of a pain was observed even if the images of nature are transmitted via movies, pictures, or sound recordings.

- A simple view of trees in hospitals reduces postoperative complications. [42]

- The presence of a houseplant can improve recovery after surgery and reduce the need of painkillers. [42]

- Sunlight enhances the release of serotonin, "the happy hormone." Serotonin is known to promote feelings of peace, serenity, and satisfaction. It also eliminates anxiety, aggression, and excessive worry.

- In senior citizen and geriatric homes, residents who regularly spent time in gardens need less painkillers and antidepressants.

- Walking in the forest drastically lowers stress hormone levels. [44]

- Regularly spending time in nature protects against sleep problems. [44]

- Nature supports heart health. Scientists in Japan and Korea demonstrated that walking in the woods as well as passively observing nature reduces blood pressure and calms the heartbeat. [44]

- DHEA, a hormone produced in the adrenals, is enhanced when spending time in nature. This hormone is considered a "heart protector" substance as well as a precursor to both male and female sex hormones.

Additionally, a technique named **earthing**, also known as grounding, can promote health and raise your vibration. Earthing is based on scientific research that demonstrated that connecting to earth's electrical energy supports physical well-being. In particular, it has an impressive positive effect on inflammation.

Also, in 2004, the Journal of Alternative and Complementary Medicine reported, "Earthing during sleep resynchronizes cortisol secretion more in alignment with its natural, normal rhythm." Other studies also reported many positive results, including the following amongst others: improved sleep, decreased pain and inflammation, reduced feelings of stress, and improvements in gastrointestinal symptoms.

Earthing can be very simple and affordable, and it can be achieved in many ways: standing, sitting, lying, or walking with direct skin contact with the ground. It is as simple as finding a piece of earth or going to the beach, kicking off your shoes, and spending twenty to thirty minutes in contact with the earth. Earthing products such as shoes and bedsheets serve as a convenient alternative to maintain contact with the earth during work, rest, or sleep.

The point of this book is for you to learn sustainable lifetime practices that produce countless health benefits. As well as help you feel a "high" without the need of substance-induce highs that can negatively impact your central nervous system. A high-vibrational life is about feeling energized calmly and steadily. In contrast, a high from caffeine or other drugs is frenetic, and there is an inevitable crash after.

Remember, it is not about continually chasing high vibrations or feeling high. In general, higher vibrations are better for us, but grounding and balance is also part of our goal. We want, instead, to experience the harmonic and cohesive vibrations that are brought about by balanced living. This way of life often starts by eating an organic, fresh, mostly plant-based whole-food diet as well as disciplining your mind.

PART 4
Emotions

Sickness is the first warning that we have made a wrong judgement. A healthy person is never unhappy.
— George Ohsawa

CHAPTER 9

Emotions and Your Reality

Energy is the currency of the universe. When you "pay" attention to something, you buy that experience.
— Emily Maroutain

Emotions have a tremendous impact on both our energetic and physical bodies. They are the language of energy, and they bring into awareness unconscious beliefs. Emotions are neither good nor bad; it is our interpretation based on beliefs that cause us to judge them as such. Being in the present moment is only achieved by embracing emotions, listening to their messages, and integrating the issues of the past.

All emotions have two essential functions: they provide information and they mobilize intention. The problem is that humans do not like to feel uncomfortable, so they tend to judge difficult and unpleasant emotions as bad. Consequently, people try to avoid or change the external circumstance to stop experiencing the emotion, but *emotions are not intended to be avoided, repressed, pursued, or altered*; instead, they need to be accepted, listened to, learned from, and processed.

Emotions are meant to show you what is happening around you and where you have gotten stuck. Most of your emotions are triggered by subconscious beliefs created by your past about yourself and the world. It is never about what is happening to us and more about our interpretation. Whether an emotion works for you or against you depends on the beliefs behind it.

If you do not like an emotion you are experiencing, all you need to do to change the feeling is to accept it. Explore the message, and integrate it to the experience in the past that created it. The more you process and experience past beliefs, the clearer you become, and the more your emotions will tell you about the present real-time situation rather than replaying unfinished business. Otherwise, you will continue to experience the same feelings because avoiding it or trying to release it will not work; it will only suppress it, driving it deeper into the subconscious. The mere fact that you are judging a situation as good or bad will bring it to the existence or allow it to persist.

Therefore, do not try to change the outer world to improve your current feelings. As I said before, there is no such thing as something "out there." It is all coming from inside you. All your emotions are being transferred from your body to your aura and vice versa, and together these attract the circumstances that match the energy vibrations of the feelings you are experiencing—like them or not. However, once you process and integrate your emotions, you will notice that your energy will shift, leading you to experience different states of mind and perceptions. Consequently, improved circumstances, life experiences, and the right people will come your way.

Emotions can also directly influence how our brain controls our physiology and impacts the quality of our cells in our bodies. In fact, "Every change in the physiological state accompanied by an appropriate change in the mental-emotional state, conscious or unconscious; and conversely, every change in the mental-emotional state, conscious or unconscious, is accompanied by an appropriate change in the physiological state," states Elmer Green, a Mayo Clinic physician. [45]

Additionally, science is now showing us that our beliefs about health and aging, prayers, thoughts, intentions, and faith contribute to our health, happiness, and longevity more than our genes. In fact, "Genes account for about 35 percent of longevity, while lifestyles, diet, and other environmental factors, including support systems, are the major reason people live longer," states Blair Justice, PhD, in his book, *Who Gets Sick.* [46]

Moreover, researchers with the HeartMath Institute have shown that the human heart possesses its own brain, which continually interacts and communicates with the head brain. Between them, they continuously exchange information that influences how our bodies function. For each emotion or feeling we experience in our hearts, there is a chemical reaction created by our brain that affects the makeup of our cells. [47]

The beliefs and feelings we hold in our hearts are in constant communication with our brains, and the brain sends out either "love" chemistry or "fear" chemistry to our bodies. Chronic positive love chemistry promotes health and favorable circumstances. On the other hand, chronic fear chemistry develops illness and adverse events.

When we hurt emotionally, our pain is transmitted through our cells and our meridians and can be responsible for physical illnesses. Research suggests that chronic hurt can be responsible for heart disease and other illnesses. [48] This is the case for long-term, unresolved, negative feelings, such as fear, frustration, depression, loneliness, anxiety, and disappointment. In fact, "Study after study has shown that people who feel lonely, depressed, and isolated are many times more likely to get sick and die prematurely—not only of heart disease but from virtually all causes—than those who have a sense of connection, love, and community," says Dean Ornish, MD, director at Preventive Medicine Research Institute in Sausalito, California. [49] Therefore, changing what we believe about what has caused us pain can help heal us and even prevent heart disease and other chronic illnesses.

Additionally, the Institute of HeartMath has demonstrated that when we intentionally experience positive emotions, such as caring, kindness, or appreciation for someone or something, the heart processes these and sends out positive information through the entire body. Therefore, to live a long and happy life, we must be willing to heal the limiting beliefs that are behind our deepest hurts, since this can renew the health and vitality of our bodies.

Dr. Bruce Lipton explains that the most critical influence on the disease process is thought. He states, "The health of our cells is predicated upon the nervous system's ability to perceive environmental information and selectively engage appropriate life-sustaining behaviors accurately." He explains, "Cells, tissues, and organs do not question information sent by the nervous system. Rather, they respond with equal enthusiasm to accurate life-affirming perceptions and self-destructive misperceptions. Consequently, the nature of our perceptions greatly influences the fate of our lives." [50]

This clearly can be seen with **the placebo effect**. A minimum of one-third of all medical healing is associated with the placebo effect. [51] Studies have shown the placebo effect to be influential in treating diseases, like depression, asthma, and Parkinson's. In fact, science has seen placebos work so well, particularly when treating depression, that psychiatrist Walter Brown of the Brown University School of Medicine has suggested that placebo pills should be the primary treatment for patients with mild or moderate depression. Studies have shown that in more than half of the clinical trials for the six leading antidepressants, the drugs did not outperform placebo pills. [52]

Additionally, a fascinating landmark study demonstrated that people with osteoarthritis improved equally well, regardless of whether they received a real surgical procedure or a placebo surgery. From the research abstract: "In this controlled trial involving patients with osteoarthritis of the knee, the outcomes after arthroscopic lavage or arthroscopic debridement were no better than those after a placebo procedure." [53]

In another study a group of people were told they were being exposed to poison ivy. In reality, they were exposed to a harmless plant. The results were amazing. The group reacted as if they had poison ivy applied to their body. The expectation of a reaction was enough for a rash to break out as well as itching and boils. The researchers also reversed the experiment; the group did get exposed to poison ivy, but they were told that it was a harmless plant. Even though they were all allergic, less than one in six reacted to the poison ivy by breaking out into a rash. [54]

These are only a few of the many studies done on the placebo effect that show that our beliefs have a powerful influence on our bodies. On the other hand is negative thinking; this is called the **nocebo effect**. The nocebo effect can be as powerful as the placebo effect, but in the opposite direction, and can damage your health and your life. Your beliefs act as if you were wearing dark sunglasses, changing how you see your life and the world, and your biology adapts to those beliefs. [50] As I said earlier, positive or "love" chemistry creates healthy cells, and negative or "fear" chemistry creates unhealthy cells. If you clear the beliefs that are causing you to be uncomfortable, you can have a healthy and happy life.

Every emotion or feeling that you have resonates with a specific vibrational frequency. These vibrations are measured on a scale of fast to slow. Emotions such as appreciation, joy, and excitement are high vibrational frequencies. Feelings such as anger, frustration, and guilt have a low vibrational frequency.

These vibrations get passed to our aura, where they always attract the circumstances that match those vibrations into our lives. Therefore, to experience what we call favorable conditions, all you must do is hold high vibration emotions as much as you can, thereby inviting similar high vibration experiences to come into your awareness.

Alternately, if you hold a lower vibrational emotion, such as anger or frustration, for long periods of time, then you are more likely to attract more of the same into your life. The following image shows each emotion and where they fall on the scale of high or low vibration. This graph is based on Esther Hick's work with Abraham, in her book *Ask and It Is Given.*

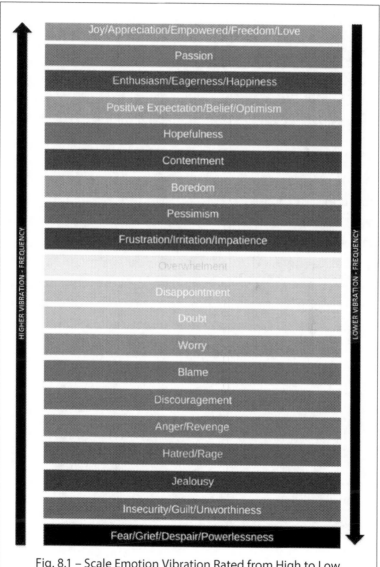

Fig. 8.1 – Scale Emotion Vibration Rated from High to Low

As Esther explains, when you are encountering a situation that causes you to be at the lower spectrum to "raise your vibration," it is best to engage in activities that will help you travel through the emotions from one level to the next, instead of trying to jump to the top. For example, if you are feeling angry, it would be easier to achieve a vibration that resonated at discouragement than it would to shoot to feeling joyful and empowered. From discouragement, you could then reach for blame, followed by worry, and then continue up one step at a time.

This technique works wonders to help you raise your higher vibration temporarily, so you can minimize attracting adverse events. However, the underlying cause is still there, and you will want to work clearing the limiting beliefs that created the emotion to begin with. Otherwise, you will eventually find another trigger that will lower your vibration; consequently, you will need to raise your vibration once more. Ultimately, to stop attracting these triggers, you want to engage in activities that can help you clear your limiting beliefs.

CHAPTER 10

The Energetics of Emotions

It isn't about the words you say. It's about
the energetic message you send.
— Pete Carroll

The energy of our emotions is also classified within the five-element system described in chapter 7. A set of emotions falls within each element, and they impact the organs and the energy flow of the meridians associated with the element. As you can see in table 10.1, the core emotional energies include the emotion of healthily balanced synergy and the emotional response to stress (out of balance). Consequently, if there is an elemental imbalance caused by emotions, this energy imbalance travels up the chakras and aura, impacting the health and circumstances that we attract to ourselves.

The good news is that we can curve these emotions not only by changing our beliefs, but also by balancing the five-element energies, using the generating or controlling cycles explained in chapter 7. This can be done with food, changing our behavior, toning an organ, or balancing the energy in a meridian. Once the elements are balanced, this can trigger a change in our emotions, beliefs, and external circumstances.

Table 10.1. Harmonizing Emotions with the Five Elements

Element	Emotions	Balance	Disharmony
Wood (air) Liver and gallbladder	Assertion. The liver is often likened to making long-term plans and strategies. At the same time, the liver is responsible for establishing a smooth flow in the body and emotions. **Derived emotions:** anger, bitterness, guilt, hatred, resentment, depression frustration, indecisiveness panic, feeling taken for granted	When the liver is harmonious, a person tends to be calm, with clear judgment, and capable of decisive action. It also includes self-assertion, motivation, the will to become, creativity, responsibility, the ability to respond appropriately, and kindness.	A classic indication of liver disharmony is emotional difficulty related to anger. Typically mood swings, as well as emotional excesses, may be associated with liver disharmony. Anger and frustration may change into a range of distressed emotional states, from the excess manifestations of irritability, impatience, resentment, animosity, belligerence, indignation, bitterness, and vengefulness, to the expressions of guilt, self-blame, lack of motivation, apathy, boredom, impotence, and depression. Starting many projects or tasks without completing them is also associated with a liver disharmony.
Fire Heart and small intestine	Joy. This is not to confuse joy with happiness; you can think of it more as enthusiasm for living.	When fire is in harmoniums, a person experiences happiness, self-confidence, and compassion.	The extreme emotions of fire are overjoy or overexcitation and shock/fright. These are stressors to the heart. Change is stressful. Whether it is a negative stress, such as the heartbreaking end of a love relationship,

Table 10.1. Harmonizing Emotions with the Five Elements

Element	Emotions	Balance	Disharmony
Earth Spleen, pancreas, stomach	The balanced or synergic emotion of the earth element is sympathy and empathy. **Derived emotions:** anxiety, despair, disgust, nervousness, worry, failure, helplessness, hopelessness, lack of control, low self-esteem	Earth harmonious states are consideration and recollection. This is the energy of stepping outside of self-interest, with genuine concern for others. This emotional-spiritual inclination of earth is concerned with deep, feeling connection.	Worry or too much concern, pity or too much sympathy, and pensiveness or excessive thinking and reminiscence are the extreme emotions of the earth phase. The spectrum of hyperactive distress includes overthinking, worry, brooding, selfishness, self-absorption, anxiety, and obsessiveness. Mental fatigue, poor concentration, forgetfulness, indifference, blaming, victim mentality, and alienation are some of the distressed responses in the deficient earth energy.
Metal Lungs and large intestine	The metal element is concerned with allowing/receiving and releasing. **Derived emotions:** crying, discouragement, rejection, sadness, sorrow, confusion, defensiveness,	When metal is harmonious, a person is concerned with openness, receptivity, independence, and nonattachment.	The extreme emotions of metal are grief, sorrow, and lamentation. These are painful emotions arising from loss. The all too common dysfunctional response, leading to distress, is to cling to the suffering, hold on tightly and not let go of the past, or shut down and not feel at all. The distressed

Table 10.1. Harmonizing Emotions with the Five Elements

Element	Emotions	Balance	Disharmony
	grief, self-abuse, stubbornness		states of metal are excessive grieving, stoicism, defensive pride, possessiveness, jealousy, envy, and greed. The deficient spectrum includes self-pity, hypersensitivity, denial, withholding of emotion, deprivation, despondency, and oppression.
Water Kidneys and bladder	Water contains the life principle of flow, adaptability, and flexibility, but also the qualities of power and form. **Derived emotions:** blaming, dread, fear, horror, peeved, conflict, creative, insecurity, terror, unsupported, wishy-washy	When water is harmonious, a person can go with the flow, follow his or her dreams (purpose), and adapt to changing circumstances without any issues. They also are able to exert caution when it is appropriate.	Unreasonable fear is often listed as the emotional aspect of water. The synergic feelings of the water phase are apprehension, resolution, volition, and trust. In distress states, the excess spectrum includes bravado, audacity, foolhardiness, superiority, suspicion, mistrust, and paranoia. The range of deficiency manifestations includes inadequacy, timidity, inferiority, fearfulness, panic, and phobias.

For example, if the kidneys are out of balance, a person often feels scared, frightened, and fearful. The person can be hypersensitive, mistrusting, and even paranoid. To resolve this imbalance, we can minimize water energy by making the mother element stronger, which in this case is metal. This can be corrected by eating certain foods, such as brown rice, onions, and radishes, or practicing any other of the recommendations listed under the metal element, such as being more open and receptive and practicing nonattachment. Alternatively, a person can practice Qigong exercises to balance the energy of water element.

According to this theory, there are seven main human emotions, and all others derive from them: joy, anger, anxiety, melancholy, sorrow, fear, and fright. These emotions are humans' responses to their beliefs of external environment. In small amounts they do not cause any physical ailments, but in large quantities and over prolonged periods, they can affect the proper functions of a person's internal organs and consequently also cause energy blocks on their energetic anatomy.

To the ancient Chinese and Japanese, one human emotion can be curbed using another emotion, based on the controlling cycle of the five elements. For example, joy (fire) can overcome anxiety/sorrow (metal), which in turn can overcome anger (wood). Anger (wood) can overcome melancholy (earth), which in turn can overcome fear (water). To do this you will have to use the controlling or creation cycle explained in chapter 7.

Once you identify which element is deficient and in excess, you can balance the energy by using many of the tools listed in part 5 of this book, such as acupuncture, acupressure, food, and flower essences.

PART 5
Understanding Your Subconscious

The only path by which another person can
upset you is through your own thought.
— Joseph Murphy

CHAPTER 11

Uncovering Your Limiting Beliefs

You begin to fly when you let go of self-limiting beliefs and allow your mind and aspirations to rise to greater heights.
— Brian Tracy

Be aware that you do not need to know the specific limiting beliefs you have or the reason behind them in order to heal them. In fact, by trying to understand the reason you are experiencing a situation, you can make it worse. Since most of your beliefs are unconscious, the intellect can interfere by trying to rationalize the perceived problem. Not only that, but you are also trying to solve a problem with the same mindset (beliefs) that created it to begin with, so you may not get to the real answer. Therefore, once you have identified a perceived problem, it is best to work with a clearing technique, like the ones described in chapter 12, and allow your higher self to take care of the details.

However, if you feel called to know your limiting beliefs, our subconscious is constantly communicating with us through symbols, people, and emotions. Therefore, techniques like dream interpretation and tarot cards can be useful to help interpret what is beneath the surface. Once identified, limiting beliefs can be cleared up using the energy medicine techniques covered in chapter 12.

The following are a few techniques that can be helpful in revealing your subconscious beliefs.

Look at What's Not Working for You

Now you know that everything in your life—health, people, events, and relationships—is a reflection of your subconscious mind. The easiest way to tell what your limiting beliefs are is by observing what's not working in your life and discovering what belief is behind them. These are the steps in this process:

1. In a notebook or journal, create a list of your perceived problems. There are seven important areas in your life that you may want to consider as you begin to define your problems.

   a. Personal: what you want to do, be, or have

   b. Relationships: friends, family, lovers, coworkers

   c. Health: wellness, fitness, body image, etc.

   d. Career and education: job, school, career

   e. Recreation: sports, hobbies, fun, vacations, etc.

   f. Financial: income, savings, investments, etc.

   g. Contribution: charities, community service, etc.

Designate a page for each category, and write what's not working in your life or anything that triggers a negative emotion under each category. See if you can remember when you had your heart broken in each category from different periods in your life and write it down.

2. The first strategy to discovering your limiting belief is in questioning your emotions.

   a. Read each one, and ask yourself, "How do I feel about it? Anxious? Angry? Hopeless?"

   b. Go back to each moment. Allow the memory to inform you and notice how you feel.

   c. Stay with those emotions and feelings, and acknowledge them for a moment. Feel it in your body. You'll find the limiting belief right beneath it. Scan your body for any pain or intense sensation you experience when you focus on that, and describe the location of it in your body. Describe its shape, color, temperature, and texture.

   d. Ask yourself, "What is this emotion telling me? Or why do I feel [emotion]?" For example, anxiety might be saying, "What will people think of me?" You might feel anger because you think, "Life isn't fair to people like me." The feeling of hopelessness might come out as, "I'm just not strong enough or smart enough to figure this out."

      i. Let yourself go back to the first time you can remember ever feeling this way.

      ii. Where were you?

      iii. How old were you?

      iv. Who is around you?

      v. What is happening?

      vi. What did you decide about what happened to you?

      vii. What stopped the pain?

      viii. What have you created over time that has made you safe? When you do those things now, how does it feel?

      ix. Was there a limiting decision you made or a limiting belief you took on there?

3. The second strategy is very simple but effective; it is the "fill in the blank" method.

    a. Select from the list a situation you're struggling with (e.g., "I can't start a coaching business") and add the word "because" at the end of it. Finish the sentence without judging your answer. An example is, "I can't start a coaching business **because I will never make enough money as a coach.**"

    b. What you say after the word "because" will give you a sign as to what your underlying limiting belief is. In this statement, the limiting belief is "I will never make enough money as a coach."

    c. Do this several times for the same problem, and write down your answer each time. Write down the first thing that comes to mind. If you do not overthink it, it can help you reveal your unconscious beliefs surrounding the topic you selected.

Dream Interpretation

Dreams are meaningful and should not be ignored. Carl Jung explained dreams as a "window into our unconscious and a representation of our deepest desires and anxieties." [55] Every dream has a unique meaning, and the dreamer can only be the one to interpret it. The reason being is our dreams are not often literal, and they communicate to us using symbols. Some symbols are universal, and their meanings can be recognized by many. However, **the ultimate interpretation of the symbol should come from the dreamer.** In other words, the meaning of the symbol is whatever it represents to the person has dreamed it. For example, let's say white symbolizes happiness to you. Seeing yourself in white could mean some event that would lead to happiness. But if white represents a color of sorrow for you, then seeing yourself in white could be a warning of some sorrow.

Therefore, when interpreting a dream, always ask, "What does [symbol, e.g., fork in the road, a dirt path] means to me?" This concept also applies to the people you see in your dreams. Your own dreams are about you, no matter who is in your dreams. The person in your dream is representing a characteristic or personality trait that reminds you of you. So ask yourself what you like or dislike about this person. That is usually a part of yourself that you want to disown or nurture.

For that reason, interpreting dreams is not about looking into a dream dictionary from A to Z, saying a dog means this and a shoe means that. Instead it is about being able to see how all the symbols and feelings in your dream tie together within the dream, and sometimes even through a sequence of dreams and your current life experiences.

To interpret your dreams, you need to remember them, a process that is difficult for many people. However, with conscious effort, you can remember more of your dreams and recall them in greater detail. These are a few techniques you can use to recall your dreams:

1. Before going to bed, set the intention that you are going to remember your dream.

2. Go to bed at the same time every night, and get up at the same time every morning.

3. Get between seven and eight hours of sleep each night.

4. Wake up slowly, with minimal movements, as opposed to jolting out of bed when the alarm sounds.

5. Concentrate on remembering your dream as soon as you wake up.

6. Stay in the same position as you awoke, and try to recall as much about your dream as possible before you think about anything else. Think about it from start to finish.

7. While you're remembering, direct your gaze on the first object you see as you open your eyes. Look at the object; focus on it. That object will most often take the inexplicit recollection of your dream to a place in your memory, where it is easier to remember details. A doorknob, a light bulb, or a lamp, for example, will help you to bring to memories of what you had encountered while sleeping.

8. Keep a dream journal next to your bed, and take detailed notes about your dreams as soon as you wake up.

Record your dream in your dream journal. Try to be very descriptive, and write down as much as possible about your dream, including things such as colors and shapes, location, weather, plot, people, overall emotion, and other symbols you may recall. If you can remember conversations, write those down first, as words are the most natural things to forget in dreams.

If you can't recall anything about your dream, write down the first thing that comes to mind and how you feel when you wake up. Sometimes feelings are related to a dream in some way, and as you start writing, you may begin to remember. You can also ask yourself why you are feeling the way you are feeling and write what comes up for you.

After you write your dream, highlight, circle, or underline the important symbols and note their category. This lets you easily see them when you look back at old dreams; it also helps you identify patterns. Don't edit or correct mistakes; you may strike errors with a single line. Be liberal with space; let your writing flow without artificial limitations.

Take note of all the symbols, and write an interpretation for each one of them. You can look up their universal meaning, and note what each symbol means to you. You can use *The Book of Symbols: Reflections on Archetypal Images* by Archive for Research in Archetypal Symbolism (ARAS) as a reference.

Put everything together by reflecting your feelings, thoughts, and what's going on in your life. You may connect a specific action with a traumatizing memory or something with a very good memory. Always remember that dreams are not objective. Look at the symbols in your dream, and ask yourself how they make you feel. Is there any special meaning attached to a symbol in your dream? For example, if you saw your dead mother holding a ring that was passed down to you, you can think about how you feel about the ring. Maybe it makes you feel sad because it makes you miss your mother, or perhaps you feel happy when you see it because it brings good memories of her. Perhaps you are missing your mother more than usual at this time, and this is your subconscious way of reminding you that you have something left of her in your possession.

Dream Journal Example

Dream Name _____   **Date** _____

Nice ☐   **Nightmare** ☐   **Recurring** ☐

This dream made me feel _____

Description

Symbols	
Symbol	**Meaning**

Dream Interpretation

Muscle Testing

Muscle testing, also known as applied kinesiology, is an incredible way of getting answers from your subconscious mind. Your muscles are surrounded by the energy of your meridians; thus, if anything impacts the flow of energy, like negative emotions, low quality food and other toxic substances, your muscles will weaken temporarily. Therefore, using your muscles, we can find what emotions or substances "weaken" or "strengthen" you.

This technique became popular in the 1960s through the work of Dr. George Goodheart. Dr. Goodheart discovered that muscles would strengthen in the presence of a positive stimuli, such as a supplement like vitamin C. Conversely, he found that they weaken in the presence of harmful stimuli, like artificial sweeteners. The way he measured strength was using arm muscles. (56)

Additionally, renowned holistic healer Dr. John Diamond discovered that muscles do not weaken just in the presence of something that is tangible; he found that it also works for intangible things, like emotions such as stress, sadness, happiness, and excitement. He concluded that the body inherently knows if something is good or bad for it. (57)

Here is how you can do a muscle test exercise:

1. Ask someone to help you with this test.

2. Hold out your nondominant arm from the side of your body, at shoulder height.

3. Ask the person helping you to apply gentle pressure to your arm in the area just below the wrist, pushing it down.

4. You need to resist this pressure.
   Remember to tell your assistant that you are not wrestling; you just need to find the ideal pressure that you can resist without too much effort.

5. Check if everything is working correctly. You can test by choosing something that your subconscious mind knows to be true—for example, your name. Say your name out loud while your assistant is putting pressure on your arm. If you are doing the process correctly, and if what you are saying is true, the level of resistance should stay the same as when you tried it in step 3. This represents a **yes** answer from your body.
   You can also test a false statement to get an idea of how the resistance will change when you get a **no** answer. Your arm should get weaker and will not be able to handle the resistance as well as before. It may take a few minutes of practice for your assistant to find the right amount of pressure for you and learn to keep it the same each time.

6. Now that you've established the technique, you're ready to test some more revealing concepts. First ask, "Do I have an emotional component that is contributing to [say your health condition, event, etc.]?"

7. If the answer is yes, use table 10.1 (chapter 10) to identify the emotion. Ask, "Is my emotion in the

'wood' element?" If you get a no, move on to the next element, and then the next and the next. Stop as soon as you get a yes.

8. Now look at the emotions for that element (listed in second column), and ask one by one which emotion is causing your issue. For example, "Is my health condition caused by anger?" Stop as soon as you find the emotion.

9. You can work on releasing the emotion, limiting belief or block, with an energy medicine modality from the list discussed in chapter 12.

The most important thing about muscle testing is asking the right questions and asking them clearly. Here are other sample questions to help you figure out what emotion might be contributing to your condition or situation.

1. Do I have an emotional component that is contributing to [say your health condition, event, etc.]?

2. Do I have an emotional component that is preventing me from healing from [say your health condition] permanently and completely?

3. Is the event or incident that is blocking my healing most an event that occurred between the ages of 0-20? 20-40? And so on...

4. Am I completely willing, able, and ready to let go of this [say your situation, health condition]?

5. Is this [say your health condition, situation] distracting me from dealing with something scary?

6. Is the best way to clear [say health condition or circumstance] by using [say energy technique want to know]?

Those are just a few examples, but you can also use the muscle test for things like:

- What foods are right for you?

- Do you need to drink more water?

- What should you order from a menu?

- What face cream or other product is good for your skin?

- Is a certain supplement good for you?

- Should I start a [type of business]?

- Which energetic medicine technique should I use?

Thematic Apperception Test (TAT): Tarot and Oracle Card Reading

The TAT is a projective test like the Rorschach test and is one of the most extensively used techniques to help people discover their underlying motives, concerns, and views. It is based on having a subject look at ambiguous pictures of people and asking them to create a narrative (tell a story) of what they see; the subject narratives reveal their subconscious beliefs. Some of the questions asked for each picture include, but are not limited to, the following:

- What has led up to the event shown?

- What is happening now?

- What are the characters feeling and thinking?

- What was the outcome of the story?

There are thirty-one cards in the standard form of the TAT. Some of the cards show male characters, some female, some both male and female, some of ambiguous gender, some adults, some children, and some show no human characters at all. One card is entirely blank. Most practitioners choose approximately ten cards, using cards that they feel are useful or that they believe will support the subject's expression of emotional conflicts relevant to their specific history and situation.

The answers to projective tests often seem unrelated, but only because it is revealing a more in-depth, unconscious thought process that you are not aware of. If you complete a projective test yourself, you may not be able to directly pin the results to a type of personality or symptoms of a mental disorder; that is a therapist's job. However, you do not need a therapist to perform this type of test at home. Similar to the TAT test, you can use the images in tarot and oracle cards to bring light to valuable information that is hidden inside you.

Here is how to do it:

1) Focus your attention to your perceived problem.

2) Shuffle the deck, and draw cards from the set. The energy in your aura will draw the cards that will tell you what is going on in the subconscious.

3) Use any of the traditional tarot layouts such as Celtic, three card spread, pentagram, etc. Regardless of the layout you select, it is your subconscious that guides you to select certain cards.

4) Just as with dream interpretation, the imagery and detail on these cards will symbolically represent your question and your options. Any warnings, advice or important people will also be symbolically represented. Card combinations and repetitive symbols in the spread are like a repetitive dream.

5) Write down the symbols you see in the cards, and you can then look up their universal meaning or the definition provided by your card deck. Also write what each symbol means to you too. You can use *The Book of Symbols on Archetypal Images* as a reference.

6) Reflect on your feelings, thoughts, and what's going on in your life in order to interpret the card or combination of cards. Look at the symbols in your cards, and ask yourself how they make you feel. Is there any special meaning attached to a symbol in the card?

Your Core Beliefs Self-Assessment

This assessment was adapted from Gregg Braden's form on finding your subconscious beliefs. [21] It is super simple and quick to gain insight into your subconscious beliefs, which might have been created during your childhood. It is not comprehensive, but it might provide you with great insight into what might be driving your life. For ease of use, I recommend you write the answers in a notebook or journal.

1. In the table below, list the positive and negative characteristics of your childhood caretakers, those who cared for you in your formative years. This should include anyone, such as parents, foster parents, older siblings, relatives, etc. Use single words or short phrases. There is no need to indicate names; just list the characteristics, such as distant, controlling, loving, determined, mean, honest, etc.

	Male	Female
Negative		
Positive		

2. In single words or brief phrases, list the things that were the most important for you to receive from your childhood caretakers, even if you did not receive them—for example, love, compassion, understanding, freedom, or attention.

What Did You Want and Need Most from Your Caretakers?

3. Next, identify recurrent frustrations that you remember from your childhood. They can be as big or small as you want—for example, not getting enough attention, wanting to be heard, or needing to be recognized.

Your Frustrations

4. Now list how you handled your frustrations—for example, broke the rules or found a different source of support. Use short phrases.

How Did You Handle Your Frustrations?

5. Now let's identify your subconscious beliefs by putting it all together. Fill out the following.

   a. I sometimes attract people into my life who are [*finish the sentence with the **negative** words from step 1*].

   b. I want them to be [*finish the positive words from step 1*].

   c. So that I can have [*finish with the words from step 2*].

    d. Sometimes I prevent myself from getting this by [*finish with the words from step 4*].

Note that while this exercise can help you identify some of your subconscious beliefs acquired in childhood, it is not comprehensive and absolute. Rarely are our patterns so clearly defined that we can say this is absolutely the reason this is happening. All we are doing with this exercise is finding patterns and themes that may be impacting your life today. It will help you to be aware of how you might still be searching for the same things you were looking for when you were young.

Once you have identified your beliefs, take the time to look at your current life and find ways in which these beliefs are impacting your current relationships and circumstances. Work with energy medicine techniques to help release them.

PART 6

Encouraging Positive Energy Flow: Eliminating Limiting Beliefs and Energy Blocks

A healer's power stems not from any special ability,
but from maintaining the courage and awareness
to embody and express the universal healing power
that every human being naturally possesses.
— Eric Micha'el Leventhal

CHAPTER 12

Energy Medicine Modalities: The Power of Intention

If you want to find the secrets of the universe, think in terms of energy, frequency and vibration.
— **Nikola Tesla**

Energy healing, or healing with intent, is a traditional medicine modality that has been reported to heal many conditions successfully. These conditions include a poor immune system, anxiety, stress, depression, fatigue, panic attacks, low self-esteem, hyperactivity, hormonal misbalances, migraines, digestive disorders, chronic pain, and many more. For example, a recent study to assess whether stored or recorded energy has an influence on breast cancer cells in vitro, using energy-charged cotton and the electromagnetic recordings of healers, found statistically significant biologic changes induced by healing energy, whether by direct hands-on healing or using a recording of healing activity. They also concluded that healing intention could be captured and released, thereby potentially allowing the phenomenon to be more extensively propagated. Additionally, they found that "hands-on delivery of the healing intention is stronger than with the recording used in this study, suggesting the possibility that the recording did not fully capture the healing potential." [58]

There are many approaches to energy medicine, ranging from techniques that involve contact, like in the case of healing hands, to those that include no contact, such as in distant healing. Others include biofield energy healing, spiritual healing, polarity balancing, and movement like Qigong, yoga, and tai chi. The evidence base regarding clinical effectiveness of energy medicine therapies is strongest in symptom management for pain and cancer; this is because these are the two conditions that have received the most attention. Studies are sparser but evidence is promising for clinical populations with arthritis, dementia, and heart disease. [59]

This section of the book is a brief overview of some of the vibrational medicine techniques that may help you raise your frequency and improve your life circumstances, heal your body, and strengthen your relationships. You can use this section as a springboard to engage in these topics in detail on your own.

Most of the techniques discussed in this section originated in Eastern medicine traditions, where the main focus is to balance energy—that is, qi or life force. The characteristics and conditions of qi are vital to our well-being and compromise the essence of our state of wellness and circumstances that we attract into our lives. Thus, Eastern medicine concentrates on maintaining qi in optimal health or restoring balance.

However, remember that our physical and energetic bodies work together to change our life events. One is not more important than the other, and there are times when the best approach to improve a situation might be with the physical body. This may entail the use of herbs, essential oils, food, psychotherapy, or even conventional medicine approaches.

Always be sure that you are not using the concepts of energetic blocks as a reason to not see a medical doctor or a natural healthcare provider. Some of the energetic block symptoms can also be a sign of a serious medical condition that will need to be addressed immediately.

Acupuncture

Acupuncture is a form of Asian energy medicine, when a needle is inserted at specific points that lie on the meridians of your body. There is research that suggests that it can help relieve pain and to alleviate many health issues, like headache, high blood pressure, and muscle and nerve pain.

Acupuncture works by balancing the energy (qi) that flows thought the meridians, since it is said that illnesses is a consequence of energy imbalance.

I will not go into details of acupuncture because it should only be performed by a trained professional. However, it is a highly effective method of healing that you should take into consideration when looking for a method for healing.

Acupressure

Acupressure applies the same principles as acupuncture to promote relaxation and wellness, treat Illnesses, and balance energy flowing through the meridians. Acupressure is simply acupuncture without the use of needles.

Asian medical theory describes specific points, or acupressure points, that lie on the meridians, or channels, in your body. As I explained in part 2, when one of these meridians is blocked or out of balance, illness or negative emotions can occur. Acupressure, just like acupuncture, is thought to help restore balance. The practice of acupressure teaches reciprocity, or the ability to receive as one gives. Therefore, an acupressure treatment to another person is always an opportunity to stretch, breathe, and practice self-care.

Acupressure practitioners use their fingers, palms, elbows, or feet to apply pressure to acupoints on the body's meridians. Sometimes acupressure also involves stretching. (See Appendix C for examples.)

During an acupressure session, a person will lie fully clothed on a soft massage table or comfy and padded floor mat. The practitioner gently presses on acupressure points on your body. Some of the acupressure styles include Thai massage, Shiatsu, Zen Touch, Atmena, and Jin Shin.

You can practice acupressure on yourself. All that is required is for you to have a map of meridians such as fig. 7.3 and press on the points related to the condition that you have or do the stretches recommended for that specific meridian (for a list of meridian stretches see appendix C). However, it is best to work with a trained professional when dealing with chronic illnesses; they will help relieve symptoms and will know how to balance energy based on the five-element theory or other Asian methodology.

Listed are the most popular spots you can work on at home that are believed to improve energy flow throughout the body. To get a full effect, pressure should be applied for at least half a minute, but preferably longer. One to two minutes should work best. I prefer to apply intermittent pressure. I apply pressure for four to five seconds, stop, and then press again for four to five seconds, until one or two minutes has passed. To apply pressure, you can use your fingers or an object three to four millimeters thick, like a pencil eraser.

- **Gallbladder 20 (GB20):** This is often used for headache, migraine, eye blurriness, fatigue, low energy, and cold/flu symptoms. It is located by feeling the mastoid (ear) bone and following the groove back to where the neck muscles attach to the skull.

- **Gallbladder 21 (GB21):** It is located by pinching the shoulder muscle with your thumb and middle finger and is often used for stress, facial pain, headaches, toothaches, and neck pain. Do not use this in pregnant women.

- **Large intestine 4 (LI4):** This is wonderful for stress, headaches, toothaches, facial pain, and neck pain. It can induce labor and must never be used during pregnancy. It is located on the highest spot of the muscle, when the thumb and index fingers are brought close together.

- **Liver 3 (LV3):** This is an excellent area for stress, low back pain, high blood pressure, limb pain, insomnia, and emotional upset. It is located on your foot, about two finger widths above the place where the skin of your big toe and the next toe join.

- **Pericardium 6 (P6):** This provides relief for nausea, anxiety, carpal tunnel syndrome, upset stomach, motion sickness, and headaches and is even used for regulation of heart palpitations. It is located three finger breadths below the wrist on the inner forearm, in between the two tendons.

- **Triple energizer 3 (TE3):** This is located in the groove formed by the tendons of the fourth and fifth fingers, behind the knuckles, and is commonly used for temporal headaches, shoulder and neck tension, and upper back pain.

- **Spleen 6 (SP6):** This is good for urological and pelvic disorders, menstrual cramps, and fatigue and insomnia. Avoid during pregnancy. It is located on the inside of your leg, just above your ankle, four finger widths up your leg.

- **Stomach36 (ST36):** This is used for fatigue and depression, as well as knee pain, gastrointestinal discomfort, and to promote longevity. It is located four finger widths down from the bottom of your knee cap, along the outer border of your shin bone. If you are in the right place, a muscle should pop out as you move your foot up and down.

Knowing all these points is not necessary, you can balance the five elements by using acupressure on the meridian of the element you want to work on.

Affirmations and Visualization: The Power of Repetition and Images

Affirmations are positive statements, which affirm your desired belief, goal, or state of mind as if you already achieved it. There are two types of affirmations: action and positive. *Action* affirmations are positive statements that affirm you have achieved a goal, and a *positive* affirmation is simply a statement that affirms a positive belief about yourself or the world.

You can override your limiting beliefs using affirmations and positive visual imagery. As I said in chapter 5, the subconscious cannot tell the difference between something real or imagined. With practice imagining a different circumstance, the subconscious mind will store it as a new experience and gradually transform your belief and modify your daily behavior to match your new beliefs.

Bestselling author and leading success coach Jack Canfield explains that action affirmations should be written following eight guidelines [60]:

1. Start with the words "I am …"

2. State it in the positive; don't use the word "no."

3. State it in the present tense.

4. Keep it short.

5. Make it specific; vague affirmations produce vague results.

6. Include an "ing" action verb, such as expressing, working, etc.

7. Include a dynamic feeling word, such as enjoying, excited, etc.

8. Make affirmations for your own behavior, not other people's.

Example 1: I am looking and feeling great at my perfect weight of 115 pounds.

Example 2: I am enjoying expressing my true feelings with comfort and ease.

"An affirmation is on target when it is easy to say and makes you smile with excitement. Sometimes the excitement may be accompanied by mild discomfort. This discomfort is good, because it usually means the affirmation is beginning to motivate you toward new, more self-nurturing and self-expressive actions."

— Jack Canfield

Affirmations not only help you achieve your desire outcome, but they can also override a limiting belief about yourself and world. As stated earlier, these types of affirmations are called positive affirmations; they are affirmations that simply affirm positive beliefs about yourself and the world. They must be positive, self-affirming, self-empowering statements that uplift and inspire you. Below are examples:

- I'm loved.

- I am love.

- I trust life.

- My life is full of love and beauty.

- I believe all things are possible.

- Whatever I need to know is revealed to me at exactly the right time.

- I am healthy, whole, and complete.

- I'm always safe.

- I experience love wherever I go.

- I'm always provided for.

- I'm proud of myself.

- I'm remarkable and cherished.

The power of the affirmation increases when it is linked to a visual image and the feeling of the desired outcome. It is essential to let yourself feel—as strongly as possible—the emotions that you imagine you will feel when your desired outcome has occurred.

How to Use Affirmations

1. Repeat your affirmations three times per day. The best times are first thing in the morning, in the middle of the day, and before bedtime.

2. It is better to work consistently with a few affirmations at one time than repeat a lot of them.

3. Close your eyes, and visualize experiencing what the affirmation describes. See the scene as you would see it if you were looking out at it through your eyes—as if it were happening around you.

4. Hear any sounds you might hear when you achieve what your affirmation describes.

5. Feel the feelings that you will feel when you reach what your affirmation describes.

Flower Essences

Flower essences are not to be confused with aromatherapy (essential oils). Flower essences are liquid extracts made by the infusion of the vital essence or qi of a flower into water. They are often used to address issues of emotional well-being, soul development, and mind–body health. The essences are made by placing the fresh, dew-filled blossoms of flowers in a bowl of water. The container is then placed under the light and warmth of the sun for several hours. This process creates an energetic imprint of the etheric energy pattern of the flower in the water, embodying the healing archetype of that plant. This is called the "mother essence," and it is preserved with brandy and then diluted and potentized to form the "stock," which is sold in stores and to practitioners for them to create dosage bottles. Dosage bottles are what is often recommended to use in order to take the product.

Every flower has a different healing quality, and because each flower acts as an agent of change at a deep emotional level, they offer an excellent way to heal and grow. Some of the positive changes that flower essences can help with include feeling more positive, confident, and creative; experiencing more joy, love, and peace; being more forgiving and accepting; forming better relationships; and having more clarity, focus, and concentration. They can also help break free from limiting beliefs associated with negative emotions, such as abandonment, anger, fear, and repression. Mother Nature has given us a flower to practically alleviate or promote any emotion.

The belief behind flower essence is that the vital force of each flower resonates or matches the vibration of one or more emotion or state of mind. When we drink the water that contains the essence(s), that matches that which we need for our healing and growth; it will influence us on mental, emotional, and physical levels. Flower essences interact and work with our subtle bodies to evoke specific qualities.

Flower essences will begin working in a matter of seconds, minutes, or days. It will depend on the situation, person, and depth of the issue. The change may be very noticeable or subtle, with changes occurring over time. Nevertheless, because they trigger the body to rebalance an emotional state that is out of balance, they will have a long-term effect.

You do not have to create your own mother flower essences from scratch. Like I said earlier, you can buy the stock essences and mix your own. There are hundreds of flower essences on the market. You can start with experimenting with the stock Bach flower essence or the FES California flower essence. Both can be found online with a description of how each flower can assist you.

Below are some of my favorite essences (although you should look for flowers that match your issues):

Flower	Brand	Promotes
Grape	Spirit in nature	Love and Self-love
Corn	FES and other brands	Clears limiting beliefs
Bluebonnet	Dr. Toni's Flower Essences	Clears limiting beliefs
Cherry	FES and other brands	Joy
Walnut	FES, Bach	Eases transition
Olive	FES	Sense of well-being
Gorse	FES, Bach	Hope, optimism
Tomato	Spirit in Nature	Courage
Mimulus	FES, Bach	Strength to face everyday trials
Apple	Spirit in Nature	Peaceful clarity
Lettuce	Spirit in Nature	Calmness
Pear	Spirit in Nature	Peacefulness
Raspberry	Spirit in Nature	Kindness and compassion

How to Make Your Personal Formula from Stock Bottles

- Buy a dark 1oz (30 ml) glass bottle with a dropper for the lid. You may get this at a health food store or online.

- Add to the bottle two drops of each of the flowers you selected for your condition (from the stock bottles).

- Add to the container a teaspoon of brandy and apple cider vinegar or glycerin (to preserve) and then top the bottle up with water.

- This will be your dosage bottle; you will need to take from this bottle four drops at least four times a day, or as needed.

Because of emotions and needs changing often, it can be expensive to have all the existing flower stock bottles in your house or to keep buying them. Sometimes it is just quicker and more affordable to purchase premixed dosages specific for your issue or single flowers already in dosage bottles that you can take without having to make anything. You can find some predesigned formulas on my website at http://bit.ly/DrToniFlowerEssences (get a discount coupon in resource section of this book).

The Energetics of Foods: Tell me what you eat, and I will tell you who you are.

Biochemists, nutritionists, and other natural health practitioners focus mostly on how the foods we eat, as well as the quality of the foods, impact our physiology. While this is important to keep our bodies healthy, there is a different side of food that is rarely considered. According to Asian theories, **food is more than mere fuel. It also imparts us its life force (qi) and a living wisdom and intelligence** that exceeds the science of calories, grams, and nutrient values. In this theory it is understood that food you consume conveys the unique energetic qualities of its source– its personality and its character, such as swiftness from wild deer and being grounded from root vegetables. [61]

Food is described as possessing certain qualities, such as warming or cooling, or certain flavors, such as pungent or sweet, or acting on our body in a specific way. This information is obtained by observing the behavior of the body after food has been consumed. The nutritional value of a food is stated as a set of energetic properties that describe the actions a food has on the physical and energetic bodies. In other words, an energetic viewpoint suggests that we absorb the qualities—texture, temperature, taste, smell, look, movement, and feelings—of our food sources. From this perspective, food is used to nourish and harmonize the body, mind, and spirit. All foods have a distinct energy and specific properties that can help to balance our bodies or that create imbalance, which ultimately results in sickness.

Asian cultures view food energetics based on the electromagnetic patterns of foods and how these vibrations affect our bodies. They view food energetics in terms of frequencies, as if your body is a radio and each food represents a station. When the foods you eat are right for your body constitution and condition, the sound on the radio is clear. But when you eat foods that conflict with your body's frequency, the interference disrupts the station and causes static. In other words, your body becomes imbalanced because of a food's frequency disrupting its resonance.

Food energetics also takes into consideration a person's constitution and condition. By eating the correct foods for your constitution and condition, you're feeding your body what it needs to be in balance. For example, someone with a body constitution that is cold would benefit from incorporating into their diet foods that are warming to the body, such as cinnamon and ginger. The list below shows examples of foods based on their native temperature.

- **Cold:** banana, grapefruit, watermelon, persimmon, tomato, seaweed, seafood, salt

- **Cool:** apple, pear, cucumber, spinach, tofu, peppermint, tangerine, strawberry, lettuce, barley, wheat, orange, eggplant, radish, mung bean, sesame oil

- **Neutral:** fig, papaya, peanut, celery, potato, shiitake mushrooms, rice, milk, grape, pineapple, cabbage, beet, sweet potato, yam, soybean, egg, oysters, olive, plum, carrot, corn, pumpkin, green beans, beef, pork, honey

- **Warm:** cherry, date, chestnut, asparagus, onion, malt syrup, chicken, vinegar, brown sugar, basil, clove, rosemary, coconut, peach, walnut, green onion, squash, sweet rice, mussel, wine, fresh ginger, dill, nutmeg, spearmint, guava, raspberry, chive, leek, mustard greens, mutton, shrimp, coffee, fennel, garlic, coriander

- **Hot**: soybean, black pepper, cinnamon, red pepper, dried ginger

Additionally, food energetics is highly concerned with how the environment affects our bodies, and it encourages us to live in accord with nature, rather than trying to adapt nature to us. The focus is on how to maintain harmony within the body and between the body and the outside world. The natural cycle of the seasons has a profound effect on human growth and well-being and should live in harmony with them. This process is undertaken in part by knowing how to prepare food according to the season. [32]

Nature provides foods that are better suited for us to eat during each season. For example, during the winter our bodies need to stay warm. Thus, eating root vegetables that are often available during late fall and winter are ideal. However, there is an exception: if a person is not healthy, **balance the individual and then attune for the season** without affecting the person's internal climate. For example, a person with edema cannot tolerate salt, even though more salt is needed in the winter. Individuals with edema should not increase salt. Instead, emphasize the bitter flavor that is drying and helps in the colder season. [32]

Food energetics also takes into consideration how the energy of a food is impacted by the way that is cooked. For example,

- When a "warm" food is served raw and cold, this will have a cooler influence.

- When a "cool" food is served cooked/heated, it can have a warmer effect.

- The "hottest" forms of cooking are done at very high heat, such as when frying or grilling.

- Steaming, baking/dehydrating, braising, and other forms of "slow and low" temperature cooking are considered moderate/slightly warming.

As with everything else in the universe, these characteristics can be classified within the five elements explored in chapter 7. Therefore, we can use this system to select foods that bring energy to meridians and help harmonize our health and emotions.

Harmonizing the Five Elements with Food

The following table shows a sample of food classified within the five elements, as well as the flavor for each element, so it will be easier for you to determine what foods fall under each element, even if is not on this list.

Element	Organs	Harmonizing Food	Flavor
Wood (air)	Liver and gallbladder	Barley, wheat, rye, rising greens (leeks, onions, celery, sprouts), spring fruits	Sour
Fire	Heart, pericardium, small intestine, and triple warmer	Corn, amaranth, quinoa, leafy greens (kale, collards, dandelion), summer fruits	Bitter

Earth	Spleen, pancreas, stomach	Millet, round vegetables (squash, pumpkin, cabbage, cauliflower), late summer fruits	Sweet
Metal	Lungs, large intestine	Rice, contracted plants, roots (radish, onion, burdock, carrot), autumn fruits	Pungent
Water	Kidneys, urinary bladder	Buckwheat, beans, seaweeds (cooked), winter and dried fruits	Salty

Here is a list of the therapeutic properties of each flavor

Flavors in Asian medicine do not just mean taste, they also speak to [32]:

- Temperature (warming/cooling)

- Their action in our bodies (moistening, drying, astringent, purgative, antibiotic, dispersing, tonifying, etc.)

- Where their energy is directed in the body (up or down)

- How to use therapeutic in an organ or organ system

For example, the bitter taste of dandelion reduces heat and dampness, particularly in the liver, spleen, pancreas, lungs, and heart. Dandelion and other bitter herbs tend to direct energy inward and toward the lower part of the body.

Things to consider when looking at foods to heal and remove energy blocks are:

- On occasions, you will run into a food that is assigned a flavor that does not correspond with its taste. This is because the flavors designated to reflect the healing properties of the food. For example, green tea is considered "sour" because the sour flavor has an astringent effect on the body and green tea is extremely astringent.

- The flavors of pungent and sweet tend to be warming and direct energy outward and to the higher part of the body.

- The flavors of sour, bitter, and salty are cooling. These flavors conduct energy to the lower part of the body and inward.

- In a healthy person, the flavors should be balanced, with sweet flavor dominating because sweet is the earth element flavor, and the earth element is considered the most fundamental aspect of the body.

- A healthy person should eat mostly sweet flavor every day, which should be accompanied by small amounts of bitter, salty, pungent, and sour foods. Sweet flavor is the primary flavor of most complex carbohydrates, such as grains, vegetables, legumes, nuts, seeds, and fruit. Do not confuse sweet flavor with sugar!

- Often these primary carbohydrates will contain enough secondary flavors themselves; otherwise, condiments can be used to add the flavor.

- When health is weak, and during acute disease conditions, it is better to change just two flavors in the diet, emphasizing one and restricting a contradicting one.

- Quantity of flavors is significant. Too much of one flavor has an opposite and weakening effect. This is often seen in the use of the sweet flavor. When too much is consumed, the result is impaired digestive absorption, mucus accumulation, and blood sugar imbalance, such as with diabetes and candida.

Pungent

Properties: expansive, dispersive; when the pungent flavor has a warming energy, it stimulates the circulation of energy and blood, tending to move energy upward and outward, to the periphery of the body.

- Stimulates digestion and expels gas from the intestines.

- Disperses mucus caused by food (spleen, pancreas) and colds.

- The diaphoretic pungent foods, like cayenne, mint, elderflower, scallion, garlic, and chamomile, are used to induce sweating during a cold or other exterior condition.

- Lightens the effects of grains, legumes, nuts, and

seeds, which all have slight mucus-forming properties.

- Disperses stagnant blood and increases qi energy.

- Some of the extremely pungent flavors, such as garlic, cayenne, and mugwort can destroy and expel parasites.

- Clears the lungs of mucus conditions.

- Moistens the kidneys, which affects fluids in the entire body, and can increase saliva and sweat. The hot, pungent herbs tend to be good for cold, contracted conditions of the kidneys, warming them and relaxing them.

- Stimulates blood circulation.

- Helps clear obstructions, and improves sluggish liver function.

- **Pungent** is the flavor associated with the metal element. Therefore, it can be used to balance the emotions related to this element (see table 10.1)

- Hot pungent flavors—dry ginger and cinnamon— are good for overcoming coldness, since these herbs are deeply warming for a relatively long period, as opposed to cayenne and other peppers that are so extreme that they change to a cooling effect after thirty minutes or so.

- *Who benefits from this flavor:* Those who are sluggish,

dull, lethargic, or excessively heavy, and metal element organs.

- *Warming pungent examples:* spearmint, rosemary, scallion, garlic, all onions, cinnamon bark and branch, cloves, fresh and dried ginger root, black pepper, all hot peppers, cayenne, fennel, anise, dill, mustard greens, horseradish, basil, and nutmeg

- *Cooling pungent examples:* peppermint, marjoram, elderflowers, white pepper, and radish

- *Neutral pungent examples:* taro and turnip

Salty

Properties: cooling effect; tends to move energy downward and inward; has a "centering" earthy quality; moistens dryness; softens hardened lumps and stiffness; improves digestion; detoxifies the body and can purge bowels and promote emesis.

- May be used to soften lumps, like hardened lymph nodes, cataracts, and another knotting of muscles or glands.

- Can be used internally for constipation, abdominal swelling, and pain, and externally for impure blood conditions with heat signs, such us most skin discharges, sore throat (gargle), and gum disease.

- Descending cooling nature of the salty flavor attunes a person to the colder seasons and climates and can be used progressively more during fall and winter.

- Considered an appropriate flavor for the spleen and pancreas, where it strengthens the digestive function.

- Forties a weak heart–mind, and improves mental concentration (grounding).

- **Salty** is the flavor associated with the water element. Therefore, it can be used to balance the emotions related to this element (see table 10.1)

- *Most beneficial for:* moistening and calming the thin, dry, nervous person (grounding)

- *Contraindicated:* Must be significantly restricted for those with damp, overweight, lethargic, or edemic conditions and those with high blood pressure; except with seaweed, because this speeds up metabolism. Salt should be used in moderation or sparingly by aggressive individuals.

- *Examples:* salt, seaweed (kelp, kombu, bladderwrack, dulse, etc.); barley and millet, although they are considered primarily sweet; products made with substantial amounts of salt, like soy sauce, miso, pickles, umeboshi, and sesame salt

Sour

Properties: cooling effect; causes contraction and has a gathering, absorbent, astringent effect that helps prevents or reverse abnormal leakage of fluids and energy, and to dry and firm up tissues.

- Used in the treatment of urinary dripping, excessive perspiration, hemorrhage, diarrhea, and weak, sagging tissues, including flaccid skin, hemorrhoids, and uterine prolapse.

- Sourest flavors are found in black and green tea, and blackberry leaves can be classified as astringents.

- Most active in the liver, where it counteracts the effects of fatty, greasy food; it functions as a solvent and breaks down fats and protein.

- Helps in digestion to dissolve minerals for improved assimilation, and can help strengthen weak lungs.

- Proper for the heart–mind, as it plays a role in organizing scattered mental patterns.

- Lacking in the current modern diet.

- **Sour** is the flavor associated with the wood element. Therefore, it can be used to balance the emotions related to this element (see table 10.1)

- *Contraindications:* for those with dampness, the heaviness of mind and body, constipation, and constrictions (use sparingly); do not eat too much sour food if you have diseases of the tendons or ligaments.

- Most sour foods also have other prominent flavors, such as the following:
  o Sour: Hawthorn berry, lemon, lime, pickles, rosehip, sauerkraut, sour apple, sour plum

  o Sour and sweet: adzuki beans, apple, blackberry, cheese, grape, huckleberry, mango, olive, raspberry, sourdough bread, tangerine, tomato, yogurt

  o Sour and bitter: vinegar

  o Sour and pungent: leek

Bitter

Properties: cooling effect; causes contraction and encourages the energy of the body to descend; reduces the *excessive* person (robust, extroverted, with thick tongue coating, loud voice, reddish complexion, etc.); lowers fever; will also dry fluids and drain dampness; some have a purgative effect and induce bowel movement.

- One of the most underused and least appreciated of the flavors.

- Helps inflammation, infections, and overly moist, damp conditions.

- Used for constipation.

- Related to the fire element and heart. It clears heat and cleans arteries of damp mucoid deposits of cholesterol and fats; in general, tends to lower blood pressure. (Celery is specifically used for this.)

- Clears stagnancy and cools heat in the liver (usually caused by overconsumption of rich foods).

- Drains various damp-associated conditions, in the form of candida yeast overgrowth, parasites, mucus, swellings, skin eruptions, abscess, growths, tumors, cysts, obesity, and all moist accumulations of edema in regions governed by spleen and pancreas (the intestines and the flesh of the body).

- Increases intestinal muscle contractions and promotes peristalsis.

- Tonifies and vitalizes kidneys and lungs.

- **Bitter** is the flavor associated with the fire element. Therefore, it can be used to balance the emotions related to this element (see table 10.1)

- Removes mucous/heat conditions in the lungs, signified by yellow phlegm discharges. Even though the bitter flavor belongs to the heart (fire element), it is also a proper flavor for the lungs.

- *Most beneficial for:* slow, overweight, lethargic, watery (damp) individuals; also overheated, aggressive persons

- *Contraindications:* limited amounts for people who are deficient, cold, weak, thin, nervous, and dry

- *Examples for significant imbalances:* dandelion leaf or root, burdock, yarrow, chamomile, hops, valerian, chaparral, echinacea, and pau d'arco

- Most bitter foods also have other prominent flavors, such as the following:
  o Bitter: alfalfa, bitter melon, romaine lettuce, rye

  o Bitter and pungent: citrus peel (also sweet), radish leaf, scallion, turnip (also sweet), white pepper

  o Bitter and sweet: amaranth, asparagus, celery, lettuce, papaya, quinoa

  o Bitter and sour: vinegar

Sweet

Properties: Classified into full sweet (more tonifying and strengthening) and empty sweet (more cleansing and cooling like in fruits); when found in warming foods helps energy expand upward and outward in the body; harmonizing, with a slowing, relaxing effect; builds tissues and fluids of the body; tonifies the thin and dry person; acts to strengthen weakness and deficiency in general.

- Used primarily in the form of complex carbohydrates, which energize and relax the body, nerves, and brain.

- Can be used to reduce the harsh taste of bitter foods.

- Treats the cold or deficient person in the form of complex carbohydrates, such as grains, vegetables, and legumes.

- Appropriate for any season.

- Strengthens the spleen and pancreas and is also an appropriate flavor for the liver, since it soothes aggressive liver emotions, such as anger and impatience.

- Moistens dry conditions of the lungs, and slows an overactive heart and mind.

- **Sweet** is the flavor associated with the earth element. Therefore, it can be used to balance the emotions related to this element (see table 10.1)

- *Most beneficial for:* the dry, cold, nervous, thin, weak, or scattered person who needs sweet foods in greater quantity; the aggressive person, who benefits from the retarding effect of the sweet flavor.

- *Contraindications:* moderate amounts for the sluggish, overweight person, or those with damp signs, including mucus conditions; chew well, since it makes them less mucus forming and therefore has a lighter impact on digestion; too much damages the kidneys, spleen, and pancreas; weakens the bones and causes hair loss; do not overeat sweet foods if diseases like obesity, tumors, and edema are present.

- *Examples:* all the grains amongst the most important sweet foods, although quinoa and amaranth also are bitter; all legumes, dairy, and meat

- Most sweet foods also have other prominent flavors, such as the following:
  o Fruits: apple, apricot, cherry, date, fig, grape (sour), grapefruit (sour), olive (sour), papaya (bitter), peach (sour), pear (slightly sour), strawberry (sour), tomato (sour)

  o Vegetables: beet, button mushroom, cabbage (pungent), celery (bitter), chard, cucumber, eggplant, lettuce (bitter), potato, shiitake mushroom, spearmint (pungent), squash, sweet potato, yam

  o Nuts and seeds: almond, chestnut, coconut, sesame seed and oil, sunflower seed, walnut

  o Sweeteners: barley malt, raw honey (although sweet in taste, honey has a pungent, drying effect on the body after digestion and dries up damp, overweight, and mucus conditions), molasses, rice syrup, whole sugar (unrefined cane juice powder)

How to Heal and Release Energy Blocks with Food

You learned in chapter 10 how each element is associated with a pair of organs and different kinds of emotions. To change our circumstances or improve our health using food, we can look to see if a deficiency or excess of one of the elements could be contributing to physical health or emotional issue and then attempt to resolve this by adjusting our diet. According to this theory, you can bring balance and health to your body by balancing these elements, following the five element generating sequence. The following are examples of this theory.

- To increase the presence of wood energy, we might eat more steamed green vegetables.

- To experience more fire energy, we could eat more fire foods and include onions, garlic, and ginger in the dish.

- To feel more earth energy, we can experiment with more pumpkin and carrot soups and stewed apples for dessert.

- To increase the presence of metal energy, we might try more pressure-cooked brown rice, barley, and wheat.

- To experience more water energy, we can eat miso soups and bean and vegetable stews.

Similarly, we could reduce our exposure to specific element energy by eating less of the element foods associated with that element. So, if we felt too withdrawn, less metal energy foods and more fire energy foods could help. This is a concept that most Westerners, including my clients, have a difficulty understanding. My clients often ask why I am telling them to avoid or minimize certain foods that are healthy from a Western perspective. This happens because they are only looking at food for their nutritional value—the vitamins, minerals, fats, proteins, carbohydrates, antioxidants, and so forth—rather than observing the health benefits of food characterized by their energetic effects on the body and mind.

The benefit of understanding food energetics is developing a more holistic perspective on nutrition. When it comes to our health, there is a risk in focusing only on the nutritional value of food and overlooking the energetic properties.

For example, in the West, fruits are thought to be healthy because they have many great nutritional qualities, such as antioxidants that help fight cancer. They also improve mood and energy and support overall health and wellness. However, in Eastern medicine, overeating sweet, cold, raw foods like fruits are known to create dampness, which isn't a problem when eaten in moderation. With this in mind, overeating fruits can cause dampness in the body, including in the intestines, and dampness in the intestines eventually causes chronic diseases to form, like candida, a fungal infection that thrives in damp environments and can be challenging to eliminate. Also, candida causes many bothersome symptoms, such as rashes, brain fog, chronic fatigue, allergies, lethargy, and more. As you can see, if we only consider the Western nutritional value of food such as fruits, eating a lot of fruits seems to be a good thing to do for our health. However, when taking into consideration the energetic perspective of fruit, it becomes apparent that, if we want to stay healthy, we should only eat fruit in moderation.

It is important to note that the East and West worldviews are not at odds with each other. Instead, they complement each other, and together they can help us understand a fundamental principle in creating radiant, lifelong health, which is filled with balance and moderation.

Soak Your Grains, Nuts, and Legumes

The process of soaking grains and legumes, also known as culturing, is centuries old. The purpose of soaking is to help break down antinutrients, such as phytic acid, tannins, enzyme inhibitors, and hard-to-digest components of the grains, legumes, and nuts. And at the same time, it helps to release beneficial nutrients like vitamin B and minerals. Soaking also starts the sprouting process, which makes your food more alkalizing and easier to digest.

Phytic acid or IP_6 is a compound found in grains and legumes and has received a lot of unfavorable publicity lately. It is being vilified as a mineral absorption inhibitor. However, this supplement is frequently extracted from brown rice and used successfully in cancer therapy to inhibit tumor growth and cause cancer cells to go back to normal. IP_6 may also have applications in the treatment of cardiovascular disease, kidney stones, and immune system disorders. Nevertheless, you can neutralize IP_6 in grains in legumes by soaking them and discarding the soak water, sprouting, fermenting, and roasting. [32]

HOW LONG SHOULD YOU SOAK GRAINS, LEGUMES, AND NUTS?

As little as seven hours of soaking in warm water will neutralize a significant portion of phytic acid in grains and legumes and will vastly improve their nutritional benefits. Placing soaked kombu or kelp seaweed at the bottom of the pot when soaking increases the effectiveness of the process. Add one part seaweed for six or more parts grains or legumes.

Soaking is not as laborious or time-consuming as you may think it may be. It is effortless to do. All it takes is a little planning ahead, and I set my grains, legumes, and nuts to soak right before going to bed and rinse them in the morning when I wake up, making them ready for whenever I need to cook. The result is a highly nutritious and easy-to-digest whole-grain food with excellent flavor.

Hypnotherapy

Hypnotherapy is not an energy medicine tool. However, it is one of the best tools to reach and change your subconscious mind. Therefore, I felt I had to mention it briefly in this book.

Hypnotism is the induction of a state of consciousness sort of a daydreaming state, in which a person is highly responsive to suggestion or direction. Its use in therapy, typically to support modification of behavior by suggestion.

Hypnotherapists aim to induce a comfortable and receptive state (trance) in their clients to access the subconscious. By accessing the thought processes that usually remain hidden, hypnotherapists can work with clients to change the restrictive thought pattern and make room for positive development.

Scientific evidence is now showing that affirmations and hypnosis have powerful effects on human health. Recent studies led by Russian biophysicist and molecular biologist Pjotr Garjajev, show that living human DNA can be altered and rearranged with spoken words and phrases. The key to modifying DNA with words and phrases is in using the correct frequency. In these studies, researchers have successfully transmitted information patterns from one set of DNA to another using words. Researchers were also able to reprogram cells to another genome—they converted frog embryos into salamander embryos without using a single scalpel or making one incision. [62]

This work provides scientific evidence that affirmations and hypnosis have potent effects on human beings. It seems that our DNA is inherently programmed to respond to language. This research also explains why these techniques are not equally successful for all who use them. Since "communication" with DNA needs to have the correct frequency, people with more highly developed inner processes are more able to create a conscious channel of communication with the DNA. [62]

The best thing about hypnosis is that you can choose to work with a practitioner, or you can do it on your own. There are countless of hypnosis audios out there to help you overcome any of your limiting beliefs. One of my favorites is Paraliminals from Paul Scheele. You can find them on his website http://bit. ly/drToniParaliminal use this link to get discounts.

Ho'oponopono

The knowledge I'm sharing about Ho'oponopono comes from Dr. Hew Len, a psychologist that is known to have healed an entire ward of mentally ill criminals by using the Hawaiian theory and method. The word Ho'oponopono translates to "to put right, adjust, amend, or rectify." The underlying theory of Ho'oponopono is that we are all 100 percent responsible for what is happening in our lives and the lives and behavior of the people in it. Like the concepts discussed in part 2 of this book, Dr. Len says that for this system to work **we really need to understand and be clear that there is no such thing as "out there."** Everything we are experiencing is created by our inside. That's the only place where you experience problems, and that's where the fixing needs to be done. He states that our inside is full of what he calls "memories" (beliefs) that are keeping us away from the divine. The more we clear these memories, the easier it is for us to hear the divine inspiration, as well as heal our lives.

According to Dr. Joe Vitale, the ancient practice of Ho'oponopono is summarized in three basic principles:

- Everything is alive. We are part of everything, and everything is a part of us. Therefore, everything should be treated with reverence. I mean everything, from animals, the floor you walk on, your car, your chair, to the room you are in.

- Everything in your life is a reflection of you. Don't like what you see? Clean and clear it in you.

- Everything can change, and it can only be done by changing (cleaning and clearing) the inside.

At any given moment, all you are experiencing is your perception of reality. If you are experiencing a not so good feeling, it is the outcome of a subconscious belief that you need to clean (clear). The fact is divinity does not generate negative emotions. It is your interpretation that is creating a negative experience. So how do you clean? The beauty of this system is that it is super simple:

- **Be aware of your feelings**. Notice when you perceive something as wrong. This can be triggered by a thought, another person, an event, or anything else.

- **Start to clean on the feeling** by repeating the mantra "I'm sorry. Please forgive me. I love you. Thank you." Please note it's not about cleaning on the other person, the thought, the situation, or anything out there. You created, are perceiving and judging this as a problem. So you are saying this to yourself to clear it from your subconscious.

- **Repeat** this until you feel called to or if you feel better. You can always continue at another time if needed.

The basis behind Ho'oponopono is that we create everything that is happening in our lives based on our beliefs, and by repeating a mantra to ourselves, it releases the memories or programs (beliefs) that we have recorded in our subconscious. You do not have to know what the belief is or where it originated from; as soon as you perceive something as a problem, repeat the mantra to clear it.

When we are conscious that we are 100 percent responsible for our lives, then we can accept our problems as opportunities to see what is in our subconscious and to clear it. When a perceived problem appears, we can ask, "What is going on in me that I'm expressing this problem?" And then repeat the mantra:

- You say **"I'm sorry"** because you have expressed this problem into your life. With this part of the mantra, you are recognizing and accepting full responsibility for the beliefs, actions, thoughts, and emotions that have manifested into your reality.

- You say **"Please forgive me"** because you are asking forgiveness of yourself. These words are a request to make amends with your higher self and the universe.

- You say **"I love you"** because you are a perfect expression of the divine. Emit these words to the universe (god, divinity, or energy) as a form of gratitude. When you say I love you are saying "I love you for allowing me this earth experience."

- You say **"Thank you,"** for this problem has manifested into your life so you can see your limiting belief and clean it. You are showing gratitude to your higher self as well as the universe for clearing your negative beliefs, thoughts, actions, and emotions.

This mantra asks our divinity for the healing of all beliefs, thoughts, and memories that are holding us back and the lives of the people involved in this problem. Repeating these words are crucial to reaching the subconscious mind. This method does not require you know what is happening or why; you do not need to understand what is in your subconscious that created this.

In fact, it is believed that the intellect won't be able to solve the problem, since it is where the problem originated to begin with. Trying to figure it out intellectually can create more problems, since you are not only focusing on the issue, but you also do not know what else is in your subconscious that might come up. Remember, for every thought you consciously think, there are one million thoughts being processed by the subconscious! Besides, "the only problem with human beings is that they are arrogant, because that's what thinking is. This is in essence 'I know'. Wisdom is being in the void. To be thoughtless. Only by being in the void can the Light come through. As long as I have something going on in my mind the Light can't come through. The Light can only come in when the mind is cleared–in a state of silence" Says Dr. Hew Len.

Therefore, with this method, you are asking divine intelligence to solve the problem for you. And all you must do when a perceived problem comes up is clean it with this mantra. If you do not clear the limiting belief, the issues will come back as soon as they are activated again by your thinking. So, it is best to clean, delete, erase, and transform your problems into pure love by repeating this mantra.

Dr. Len explains that you can use other cleaning methods to enhance the process. For example, blue solar water is a method. Take a blue glass, any color blue, and pour water into it. Put the bottle in the sunlight or under an incandescent light bulb (not fluorescent) for at least an hour. It will solarize the water. Drink it directly, or you may cook or make tea or coffee with it. Dr. Len believes this water can heal just about any illness.

He also recommends looking at or thinking about the flower bluebell (bluebonnet), eating corn, and practicing "Ha" breathing exercises as cleansing tools. In order to do "Ha" breathing, follow these steps:

- Silently inhale to the count of seven.

- Hold for a count of seven.

- Exhale for a count seven. Release the breath with an audible sigh.

Repeat this three to seven times, or more if you like. Because this process is about clearing your mind and not working on your body, there really is no right way to count to seven—count as fast or slow as you feel comfortable.

I know this sounds too simple and too good to be true. However, cleaning with Ho'oponopono is all that Dr. Len did for four years to heal everyone in the mental ward that he worked at. The place he worked was dangerous; the patients he dealt with had committed serious crimes, like murder, rape, and kidnapping. In the end, almost everyone had healed, and only a couple of the remaining inmates were relocated elsewhere when the clinic had to close. He never met with a single inmate; he instead looked at their files and recited the mantra.

I use this modality every day to clear up whatever is bothering me. I also use solar water every day. I love it. To enhance it, I add a flower essence formula made from clearing flowers that I created. Visit my website at http://bit.ly/ClearNowFlowerEssence for more info and to buy this formula (get a discount coupon on the resource page of this book).

Learn more about Ho'oponopono and Dr. Len in Joe Vitale's book *Zero Limits*.

Magnets

Magnetic therapy is a practice that uses magnets to alleviate pain and other health issues. Recent research has revealed that acupoints in the meridians have magnetic fields. The theory behind magnetic therapy is that the magnets can balance a person's energetic anatomy, using magnets on the meridians. The use of magnets helps the body balance its electromagnetic field with the earth.

Therapeutic magnets are typically integrated into bracelets, rings, shoe inserts, mattresses, and clothing. Magnet strength is measured in a unit called the gauss. For comparison, the average refrigerator magnet is about 10 gauss. Magnets used in therapeutic products vary from about 100 gauss to 2,500 gauss.

Research shows that magnetism can have a healing effect on our bodies. According to Robert Becker and Andrew Marino in their book *Electromagnetism and Life*, specific fast-growing tissues, like tumors, are electrically negative. It has been demonstrated that their growth can slow down or regress when a positive pole is applied. Magnetism has also been known to reduce pain and inflammation, improve circulation, stimulate the immune system, promote sleep, and accelerate healing. [63]

You can also use magnets to clear emotions that are stuck in your body or are creating a block in your energetic anatomy. The best method I've see for this is in Bradley Nelson's *The Emotion Code*. It works by getting rid of emotional blocks. He uses muscle testing to identify and release trapped emotions, which were created from past adverse events, and then he releases them using magnets. It is a relatively easy and straightforward technique to learn and use on your own. I have found it very helpful and highly recommend it.

You should not use magnets if you have a pacemaker, have an insulin pump, or are pregnant.

Meditation

Practiced for thousands of years, meditation is perhaps the most crucial tool to harness the power of thought and to allow the free flow of qi, life-force energy. It clears blocks at any location in your physical or energetic body, helping you cultivate more health, peace, clarity, and happiness.

Our thoughts are often stubborn, and they quickly wander off or turn into something we don't want. Meditation helps to "discipline" them. Learning to train the brain, to slow down, focus our attention, and be aware of our thoughts and beliefs is crucial to thrive and help us eliminate limiting beliefs. Long term mindfulness meditation practice enables us to see our emotional responses when they occur rather than automatically letting them dominate our attention.

Meditation allows the mind to slow down, which allows your natural frequency to rise, as your mind is taken off anything that may have been bothering you. Meditation also enables us to move from higher frequency brain waves to lower frequency, which activates different centers in the brain. [64] Slower wavelengths equal more time between thoughts. While we are in this frequency, we can have a stronger focus (concentration) and let go.

Inspiration comes from the space between your thoughts. Thoughts are just a reflection of your beliefs and memories. The more you slow down your thoughts, the more you are living from a place of inspiration and less from past life events.

Through deep relaxation and expanding your consciousness, you discover your balance, learn to concentrate more effectively, and find you have a higher power to affect qi within your body. You can direct this qi to different areas of your body, such as the meridians, chakras, or aura. This will allow you to balance and release energy blocks. When your qi energy is balanced, it is flowing smoothly, and this leads to good physical and emotional health and favorable circumstances.

In addition to mindfulness meditation, healing and energy balancing meditation often incorporate visualization techniques. You can choose your own images to visualize or you can use guided imagery, in which you create mental pictures in response to yours or another person's instructions. For example, if you have an illness, you might be asked to vividly picture your white blood cells fighting and winning against the disease and purging the bad cells from your body, or you may imagine white light coming down from the universe and healing every part of your body.

To reap maximum benefits from meditation, it must occur regularly and often. To start seeing results, you need to practice daily for ten minutes for at least five to eight weeks. The good news is there are many ways to apply mindfulness in your everyday life, including something as simple as closing your eyes and being silent for a few minutes a day. Appendix A is a sample meditation that you can practice daily to help you increase awareness of your thoughts.

Another way meditation is used is to purposely manipulate universal energy to bring into your life your goals and desired circumstances—what is referred to these days as "manifesting." The primary manifesting premise comes from the idea that whatever we put our focus on will be created in our life. What people often forget when trying to manifest is that this holds true for both subconscious and conscious thoughts. And we now know that the subconscious holds a lot faster and holds more information than our conscious thoughts. So it is not enough to meditate and visualize what we want; we also need to work on removing our subconscious and limiting beliefs that are keeping us from the circumstances that we desire.

Simple Meditation for Manifestation

- Work with one or two goals at a time.

- Sit with your back straight and your feet flat on the ground, or you can lay down straight; do not cross your feet.

- Close your eyes.

- Start working on the meditation listed in appendix A. Once you are relaxed (about two to five minutes), you can continue with this meditation.

- Manifestation works best when your heart is open, so take a few minutes to release any blocks that can interfere with the process. You can do this by Imagining a secure box; any shape will do. Fill it with the feelings of love, compassion, and forgiveness. Or fill it with the colors that represent those feelings for you. Add to this box any emotion or situation that can interfere with your manifesting your desires. Imagine that anything you add to this box, will dissipate and leave your awareness. Then imagine closing, locking your box and putting it away.

- Take a few moments to visualize a light (any color you wish) coming down from the heavens and to fill you up with warm, positive or expansive energy.

- Imagine how your life would be if your wish were already fulfilled. How does it feel? What are the sounds around you? What are shapes around you? Where are you? What are you wearing? Notice the colors and people around you.

- Stay with these images. It may be hard at first. You might only see shapes or shadings of colors. Over time, it will become more, and you will start to see more details.

- After five minutes on your first goal or dream, you can move on to the next.

Remember that it is essential to feel the feeling of the wish fulfilled in order to bring a new belief into existence, which will create the circumstances you desire. If you can't feel it, ask yourself, "Why do you want [your desire]?" The answer might be, "It will bring me financial security." Now that you have the feeling behind what you want, ask, "In how many ways do I currently experience this [feeling]?" Once you remember those ways, you will have the feeling you want to focus when meditating. An excellent resource for guided meditations to promote energy clearing or manifesting is http://bit.ly/ DrToniHemi-Sync

Mudras

A Mudra is a hand gesture used in conjunction with breathing, meditation, or Yoga to increase the flow of energy in our bodies, promote health, and to improve mood. Each Mudra has one or more benefits. Mostly the hands and fingers are held in some position, but the whole body may be part of the Mudra as well.

One of the most well-known Mudras are the ones often performed while meditating in the lotus position. In this pose, hands are either on the knees or lap, with tips of the thumb and index finger touching or the fingers of the right hand resting on the left palm.

Another popular mudra is the Christian crossing of the fingers for prayer. Also, the "Namaste" greeting gesture (commonly used while praying). Where the hands are in front of the chest, the palms touching.

The study of Mudras is beyond the scope of this book. There are more than 100 known mudras that have been developed over the centuries. A great book to learn more about Mudras is Mudras for Awakening the Energy Body by Alison Denicola.

Qigong

Qigong (pronounced chee-gong) is an ancient Chinese exercise and healing technique that involves meditation, controlled breathing, and movement exercises. The primary premise of qigong practice is "energy follows attention." Therefore, where we place our conscious attention is where qi energy will flow and gather. Its goal through exercise and meditation is to cultivate your energy and to release any blocks. Qigong is a practice that offers methods to work with your mind, body, and spirit. These exercises focus on different parts of your being, and all lead you in the path of better health and improved vitality.

You'll find different types of qigong practices. Each is based in the way of understanding your body's energy. Some systems look at the five elements. Others use the acupuncture meridian model. Yet, others focus on activating the different tissues of the body through movements, big and small. These movements start the flow of qi throughout the body releasing energy blocks and promoting heath.

Qigong has been shown to reduce the side effects of chemotherapy. It has also been proven useful in treating conditions, such as leukopenia. [65]

A simple Qi gong technique to increase circulation and raise your vibration daily is **Qigong Bouncing**. The Chinese name for this exercise is "jumping up and down to cure 10,000 illnesses." Stagnation and congestion are believed to be significant causes of chronic disease in Chinese medicine and Qigong bouncing, as taught by Qigong Master Chunyi Lin, creator of Spring Forest Qigong, stimulates the body's lymph system, break up stress, tightness, stagnation, and congestion in the body, and increases energy flow. Here is how you do it:

- Stand with your feet shoulder-width apart and flat on the floor, knees slightly bent, and arms relaxed at your sides.

- Keep your back and head straight and your eyes looking forward.

- Gently bounce your body up and down from the knees for about 10 seconds. Bounce by coming up on the toes and then dropping down on your heels. You should feel the vibration produced travel up the long bones of the body. You can adjust the strength of the vibration by coming up higher and dropping down harder on the heels. Adjust it for what is the most comfortable for you.

- You may continue bouncing with your arms at your sides for about a minute more or move to the next step.

- As you keep bouncing, slowly raise your arms and hands to waist level and shake your hands as you bounce. Do this for about a minute or less.

- As you continue bouncing, slowly raise your arms and hands higher than the top of your head, letting your wrists relax, so they bounce up and down with the movement of your body. You can do this for several minutes or more. (This stimulates acupuncture points in the wrists that control your breathing and heart rate.)

Then slowly drop your arms and hands to your sides, slow down your bouncing, and come to a stop.

To learn more about qigong, visit Lee Holen's YouTube channel and his website: http://www.leeholden.com/.

Reiki/Healing Hands

The energy that flows through our hands has the power to heal. One of the most popular healing hands techniques out there is the Japanese system of Reiki. Reiki has been used for stress reduction, relaxation, and healing. Like any other healing hands technique, Reiki is administered by channeling universal life energy and "laying on hands" on the person who is being treated. Energy from the practitioner is then transferred to the client and promotes energy balance.

There are five Reiki principles that we can reflect on to add balance and perspective to our lives:

Just for today, do not be angry.
Just for today, do not worry.

183

Just for today, be grateful.
Just for today, work hard.
Just for today, be kind to others.

These are spiritual guidelines that enable you to work on yourself each day, and if you fall short, you can simply try again the next day.

Anyone can learn Reiki. However, the system requires that a practitioner be attuned and that knowledge be passed down by Reiki master teacher to the student. The belief is that the attunement process opens the crown, heart, and palm chakras and creates a special link between the student and the Reiki source.

Reiki is somewhat a proprietary method that needs to be taught by only a Reiki master teacher. However, universal energy is available to all of us; you do not need a special degree, complicated training, special symbols, expensive equipment, or unusual qualifications to tap into it. After all, "energy flows where intention goes." Your intention is powerful and perhaps more important than any energy healing technique you use.

You can use your hands to balance your energy, without being a trained professional. However, before attempting any healing work, set an intention to heal or release an energy block, and complement it with the power of focus, presence, and imagination.

Simple Steps to Practicing Healing with Your Hands

- Ground yourself through meditation or any other relaxation technique. Make sure you are not angry or upset before starting. You can play relaxation music to help you ground you.

- Set the intention to send universal healing energy to yourself or others.

- Lay your hands on the person you are working with or on you if working on yourself.

- Imagine universal energy coming down through your crown chakra, down to your hands. You can choose the color of the energy based on your intention— for example, red for root chakra, purple or white for healing or spirituality, pink for love, etc. The most common colors used are gold and white, to represent universal energy.

- Focus on the person's healing and well-being while you have your hands on them. Imagine light, color or energy flowing from your hands and into the body of the person you are working on.

- To enhance the effect, you may also hold or place healing stones on the person you are working with.

Sound Therapy

According to leading expert Jonathan Goldman, director of the Sound Healers Association, the premise behind sound therapy is that the vibration of sound projects the correct frequency to that part of the body that is vibrating out of harmony and makes it vibrate back into its normal, healthy rhythm, restoring it to a condition of health. For example, research at MIT has found that a low-pitched buzz accompanied with strobes of light can clear Alzheimer's plaque and recreate brain waves lost from the disease, which in turn improves cognitive function. [66]

Sound is so powerful that researchers use sound waves to levitate droplets of water by purely by applying sound frequencies. Liquid levitation can help scientist in several ways. For instance, researchers are now taking this technique and utilizing to detect harmful contaminants in water. In a new study, lead by Victor Contreras, from the Instituto de Ciencias Físicas UNAM, Mexico, showed how using sound waves to levitate droplets of water in midair can enhance the detection of harmful heavy metal contaminants. Such as lead and mercury in water. The new technique could lead to instruments that perform real-time, on-site contaminant monitoring. Which could help prevent future lead contamination problems and detect contaminated wastewater from industrial sites. [67]

Note that sound therapy may include music, but it does not necessarily have to include it. Sound healers use a variety of instruments, including crystal healing bowls, Tibetan healing bowls, tuning forks, bells, Aboriginal rain sticks, and gongs. Everyone's frequency is different at different times, so what sound feels right for you one day may not be the same the next. It will depend on what rate your vibration is at a particular time and what vibration and frequency you need at that moment.

Sound also promotes shifts in our brainwaves by using entrainment (the synchronization of organisms to an external perceived rhythm such as human music and dance). Entrainment synchronizes our fluctuating brainwaves by using rhythm and frequency, and it then becomes possible to shift our normal beta state to alpha (relaxed consciousness) and reach theta (meditative state) and delta (sleep). The vibration and frequency of sound can affect our whole being, including releasing blocked energy from past experiences and limiting beliefs that are stuck in our energy anatomy.

Although first discovered in 1839, a study in the 1970s showed that when one tone is played to one ear and a separate tone is played to the other, the two hemispheres of the brain join and create a third (internal) tone called a binaural beat. This synchronizes the brain, contributing to clarity, calmness, and faster communication between the mind and the body. The science of binaural beats is used by people to take the brain into various states that contribute to stress relief, concentration, help sleep, pain relief, and more.

You can also combine sound therapy with meditation. This is often referred to as "binaural beats meditation." Note that not all binaural beats music is designed for meditation and relaxation, but they do work similarly in that:

- Some binaural beats music is designed to take the brain into mindful awareness and the present moment.

- Binaural beats music is often supplemented by ambient, relaxing music, like the sound design used in meditation music.

- When listening to binaural beats, you may sit in the meditation positions because it allows energy to flow smoothly throughout your body and is conducive to attaining a relaxed state of mind.

According to Jonathan Goldman and many ancient traditions, many sounds seem to resonate and balance the chakras. Among the most popular are the use of vowels and the use of mantras. Notably, the use of vowels seems to be highly effective in balancing the chakras. Below is a chart showing the 7 chakras and their related vowel sounds. [68]

Chakra	Vowel	Frequency	Keynote	Element
Root	Uh	256 Hz	C	Earth
Sacral	Ooo	288 Hz	D	Water
Solar Plexus	Oh	320 Hz	E	Fire
Heart	Ah	341.3 Hz	F	Wood
Throat	Eye	384 Hz	G	Metal
Third Eye	AYE	426.7 Hz	A	All
Crown	Eee	480 Hz	B	All

Using your voice to sound these vowels helps balance the chakras and produces physiological benefits.

Healing with sound has been known to improve or cure many ailments, including but not limited to autism, depression, learning disabilities, developmental troubles, anxiety disorder, stress, PTSD, pain management, depression, mood swings, sadness, aggravation, anger, self-pity, high blood pressure, and other cardiac disorders. My favorite binaural beats music is created by the Monroe Institute. You can learn more about it at: http://bit.ly/DrToniHemi-Sync

Stone and Crystal Healing

Crystal healing is a technique in which crystals and other stones are used to support the body in the healing process and protect against disease. It is believed that because of their geometric patterns, crystals can tap into the universal and etheric energy and frequency. Every stone operates at a particular frequency and acts as conduits for healing, allowing positive, healing energy to flow into the body and remove any energy blocks and induce relaxation.

There are many ways we can work with stones. It is essential for you to keep in mind that energy follows intention. Therefore, you can simply hold a stone, set your healing intention, and meditate on it.

Ways to Use Healing Stones

- **Wear them:** The more you touch the stones, the more you can tap into their energy.

- **Carry them** your purse or pocket: You can feel the stone throughout the day to help ground you.

- **Meditate:** They help you connect with your higher self. Also, if your meditation purpose is to heal or manifest something, you can hold the stone that relates to your intention—for example, malachite for healing or citrine for abundance.

- **Add them to your bath water:** Not all crystals are meant to be in the water, but some do dissolve in water. Check first before adding it to your bath. Rose quartz works excellent in a bath, for it promotes nurturing self-love.

- **Lay them around your house**: You will not only pick up on their energy; some stones will even clean the energy of your home.

- **Add them to your drinking water.** To help you promote spiritual and physical health. For example, use rose quartz to develop a sense of love. Note that some crystals and stones are not safe to put in water, some will dissolve, and others can be toxic. For instance, tiger's eye contains asbestos. Do your research before you add a crystal to your water. The safest crystal for water is clear quartz.

- **Add to massage or body oils.** You can add a crystal or two to the bottle of your favorite oil and apply it to the skin before meditating or when needed.

- **Create a crystal essence.** Like flower essences, an effective way of using the energies of specific crystals and gems for transformation is to make them into essences. To create them use the same directions as discussed in the flower essences section of this book.

Commonly Used Crystals

Crystal	Meaning/Use
Clear quartz	It amplifies your intention and any other stone. It has powerful cleansing effects and the ability to counteract negative energy blockages.
Selenite	It cleanses and promotes flow of energy; it is said it clears the aura.
Amethyst	It is known for its spiritual properties, it boosts inner strength and spiritual guidance. It is great for enhancing meditation practice.
Citrine	It harnesses the power of the sun. It helps bring your intention to reality. It is a wonderful stone for manifestation. It also promotes a positive outlook and stimulates the mind.
Rose quartz	It attracts and supports unconditional love.
Smokey quartz	It is grounding and helps focus on the current moment. It dissolves negative energies and emotional blocks.
Tiger's eye	It focuses energy for a specific challenge and promotes a positive outlook.
Black Tourmaline	Classified as a semi-precious stone, is revered as a premier talisman of protection and guards against radiation and environmental pollutants being excellent EMF neutralizer.

Tapping

Like acupuncture and acupressure, tapping focuses on the meridian points, to restore energy balance and relieve symptoms or blocks that negative emotions or beliefs might have caused. Emotional freedom technique (EFT) has been known to help reduce short-term or chronic stress; reduce muscle tension and joint pain; decrease fatigue and boost energy levels; decrease headaches; eliminate emotional problems, such as low self-esteem, depression, and anxiety; improve athletic performance, focus, and coordination; and promote quality sleep. However, since it is removing any block caused by a chronic emotion, it can practically alleviate any condition created by that emotion.

The basic technique requires you to concentrate on the negative emotion at hand: a fear or anxiety, a bad memory, a health problem, or anything that's bothering you. While maintaining your mental focus on this issue, you will use fingertip tapping to apply pressure to the acupoints. The EFT tapping sequence is the methodic tapping on the ends of nine meridian points:

- Karate chop (KC): small intestine meridian

- Top of the head (TH): governing vessel

- Eyebrow (EB): bladder meridian

- Side of the eye (SE): gallbladder meridian

- Under the eye (UE): stomach meridian

- Under the nose (UN): governing vessel

- Chin (Ch): central vessel

- Beginning of the collarbone (CB): kidney meridian

- Under the arm (UA): spleen meridian

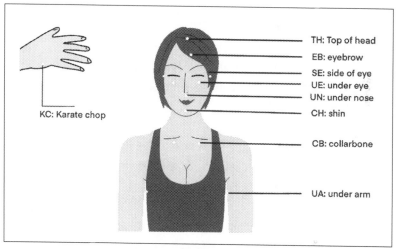

Fig. 12.1 EFT tapping points

The Simple Version of EFT Steps

- Identify your issue (could be health or emotional).

- Ask yourself how intense the feeling is on a scale from zero to ten.

- Set up the statement that is going to reflect your issue this way: "Even though I [fear or problem], I completely love and accept myself."

- Start tapping. Start by tapping the karate chop acupoint, while simultaneously reciting your setup phrase three times. Tap each following location a few times in this order: eyebrow, side of the eye, under the eye, under the nose, chin, beginning of the collarbone, under the arm.

- While tapping the points, recite a reminder phrase to maintain focus on your problem emotion. If your setup phrase is, "Even though I'm angry that my mom is sick, I deeply and completely accept myself," your reminder phrase can be, "This anger I feel." Recite this phrase at each tapping point. Repeat this sequence two or three times.

- At the end of your series, test the intensity. Rate once more how you feel on a scale from zero to ten. If you haven't reached zero, repeat the process.

There are several tapping modalities and even different methods within the same system. EFT resources include Nick Ortner website at https://www.thetappingsolution.com and the book *The Heart and Soul of EFT and Beyond* by Phillip and Jane Mountrose.

PART 7

How to Use Energy Medicine

When all your energies are brought into harmony, your body flourishes. And when your body flourishes, your soul has a soil in which it can blossom in the world. These are the ultimate reasons for energy medicine— to prepare the soil and nurture the blossom.

— Donna Eden

CHAPTER 13

Which Tool Should I Use?

Every disease is curable, except when life energy is depleted.
— Julia H. Sun

Now that you read about some of the energy medicine techniques that are available to help you eliminate limiting beliefs and release energy blocks, you might be wondering which method is the best for you. The answer is it depends. There is not a single modality that works for everyone or a unique modality that works all the time for the same person.

I have found the best approach is to clear any potential energy blocks every day. The first thing I do in the morning and the last thing I do before I go to sleep is a seven-minute chakra clearing meditation from Jonathan Goldman, followed up by a twenty-minute meditation on manifesting. I then do seven to ten minutes of sound therapy, while I recite the Ho'oponopono mantra. If something happens during the day that I perceived as a problem, no matter how big or small, I recite the mantra a few times. I also drink solar-infused water daily, wear crystals, and take flower essences as needed.

I recommend you choose a modality, depending on your current situation and how you are feeling at the moment. You can also use muscle testing to determine which technique is best for you at the moment. In other words, you will select based on what both your energetic and physical bodies need at the time, and this can extend beyond energy medicine.

Finding balance means looking after yourself physically, mentally, and emotionally and taking responsibility for your own condition. There will be times where your physical body has an immediate need, like in the case of pain, heart attack, food allergies, or if you are bleeding, and in those times, it may make sense for you to resort to conventional medicine, change your nutrition, or take herbs to resolve your symptoms. Remember that working on your physical body also impacts your energetic body, so do not get discouraged, any change you make at the physical level will eventually trigger a change at the energetic level.

After the symptom has cleared (or while is clearing), you can use energy medicine to get to the underlying belief that is causing your issue. There will be other times where your situation is not as urgent, or it will be at a level where energy medicine can be your first choice.

For example, if you have been diagnosed with diabetes, the immediate need will be to attend to your physical body by making corrections to your diet, exercising, etc. This will start the healing process. However, to get to the root of the problem, you will need to address the underlying belief that led you to develop the condition to begin with. Otherwise, you will not eliminate the situation entirely, and if you do, another similar circumstance will arise. I see this often in my clinic: My clients will get better with diet and the herbal formulas I give them, but if they do not work on the beliefs that originated the condition, then a few months or a year later, they come back with a different condition that they need help with. It is a never-ending cycle until the belief has been cleared up. This is because physical illness and the negative events in your life reflect energy blocks in your energetic anatomy, caused by emotions or choices you made based on your beliefs.

Therefore, a multidimensional approach to health, happiness, or success incorporates working on all levels of your consciousness—both your physical and energetic bodies. Take it one step at a time, so you will not be overwhelmed with all the changes you will need to do. It is okay if you must work on the physical body for a few months. Take the necessary time to eliminate the immediate symptoms.

Work on eliminating the belief that is behind your undesired circumstance when you feel you are in a place mentally, where you can focus on the underlying cause. This could be right from the start or later in the process; there is no right time. When you feel ready or called to do so, that is the right time.

Know that you do not need to know the reason or belief to heal or change a circumstance. It is our intellect ("or beliefs") that tells us we need to understand the problem. You can start clearing the belief just by doing one or several of the following:

- Reciting the Ho'oponopono mantra and letting spirit take care of the belief for you.

- Drinking solar-infused water.

- Taking a flower essence daily that has the qualities to improve the condition you are experiencing.

- Practicing EFT, while focusing on the current issue.

- Meditating or using sound therapy for clearing your chakras or belief.

- Eating foods that promote energy flow in the meridian that is blocked.

Regardless of what is happening in your life and the method you use to clear a belief, you will benefit from having a daily practice that involves some form of energy medicine, such as meditation, carrying crystals, or qigong. You can use different modalities as problems arise and you need them. Here are suggestions for when you can use each modality:

- Daily: eat high frequency food, practice qigong, meditation, sound therapy, yoga, Ho'oponopono, wearing crystals

- When an issue arises: acupressure, acupuncture, flower essences, food, EFT, sound therapy, Reiki, magnets, qigong, guided meditation, crystal healing, Ho'oponopono

Self-discovery is a lifetime's work. It is reasonable to be happy with some parts of your life and not so happy with others. This is a cycle that will repeat for as long as you are in this world. Your dissatisfaction with circumstances and people in your life are gifts that provide clues of what limiting beliefs you need to work on. Once you are aware of the problem, all you have to do is pick one of the tools in this book.

No more blaming or complaining—take 100 percent responsibility for the problem, pick a tool, and work through the issue. It does not matter which tool you choose; what is more important is that you believe the modality will help you. Your belief will be enough to change the circumstance. After all, **you create your life and events based on your expectations.**

CHAPTER 14

Key to Manifesting Your Desires

Within all of us is a divine capacity to manifest
and attract all that we need and desire.
— Wayne Dyer

A lot of the concepts that were covered in this book align with the current popular law of attraction concepts. This is the case because, in fact, I have been in part discussing the law of attraction with terms such as:

- What you think about and focus on expands.

- Higher vibrational states (emotions) attract what we perceive as favorable circumstances, and low vibrations what we believe are adverse.

- Use meditation to visualize what you want to attract into your life.

- Feel the feeling of the wish fulfilled to attract what your heart desires.

- Gratitude is a powerful attractor and will transform all areas of your life.

All the concepts of the law of attraction are true. However, it can lead us to a never-ending cycle of wants and needs. There is nothing wrong with wanting a new car, a house, success, a relationship, or even a million dollars, but what happens often is that once we obtain our goal and the excitement wears off, we feel like now we need something else. This happens because even though we achieved what we desired, we did not address the belief behind it—the "why." What feeling or need did you believe you would satisfy by earning a million dollars or by starting a new relationship? That feeling or need should have been the focus of the manifestation, not the "thing" you believed you wanted. By clearing the belief that you are lacking and focusing on the feeling you want, you can attract the right thing for you to reach your desired state.

Who knows—you may have limited yourself. If you have cleared the belief and focused on the feeling instead, you may have attracted two million dollars! Or maybe you would not have attracted any money but, instead, a new belief that will allow you to feel the sense of financial security that you have been looking for—for example, "The universe always provides for me regardless of how much money I have in the bank." After all, it is also possible to have a million dollars in the bank and still feel not secure financially, to have what we believe is the perfect relationship and still not feel loved, or to have a new car and still not feel happy. It is your subconscious beliefs that create your perception of the circumstances, not the circumstances.

Again, there is nothing wrong with wanting and acquiring things. However, I recommend that you question the "why" behind it before you start the manifestation process. Moreover, **the "why" behind your desire might give you a hint of a limiting belief that may be lingering in your subconscious, and if it is not cleared up, it could interfere with your manifestation process.**

Let's say you desire to manifest a career as a life coach. You do the work, and you become a life coach. Now your business is booming, as you wanted, and you are working nights and weekends. The money is coming in like crazy. At first glance it may seem that you got what you desire, but you are still not happy.

What happened? If you had asked yourself why you want to be a life coach first, you could have discovered that what you really wanted was to have financial abundance and the freedom to work the hours you wanted so you can spend time with you family and friends whenever you want. However, you could have achieved that by focusing on the feeling of freedom and time abundance. You may have uncovered that you have a belief that says, "Life coaches are financially abundant and can provide for their family." However, you also had a limiting belief that said, "Life coaches work many hours a week to achieve financial freedom," creating the current situation that you are in now.

Once you know the "why" ask yourself in how many ways you currently experience this feeling—for example, support, financial security, love, and companionship. Take the time to appreciate those ways, and from that place of gratitude, you can focus on manifesting your desires.

What you focus on not only expands into more significant things, but gratitude is also a powerful attractor. It raises your vibration and brings you into harmony with the energy of spirit. Gratitude can immediately transform all areas of your life. Therefore, from that space meditate on the feeling of the wish fulfilled (not the thing), and let your higher self or spirit bring you what you need to satisfy whatever it is you need be it a car, a new relationship, house, financial freedom, etc.

Do not limit yourself by creating boundaries of what you believe you want. Remember, the intellect is never going to fix what you perceived as a problem because the intellect is what causes the problem or perception to begin with. Know that it is possible to manifest anything you want into your life, you can be as specific as you like. While this may be true, it is much better to focus on the feeling you want to achieve and let Spirit/Universe bring you what you want in the form that right for you.

Once you are clear on what you really want, it is time to activate the law of attraction. As a Jack Canfield–certified trainer, the method I have found that works best for myself and my clients is the following:

- Make a list of all your wants and needs, based on your ideal vision of reality.

- Convert the items on this list into SMART goals.

  - Specific: Your goal must be clear and defined, not only to you but to others as well. It should be precise and detailed and answer questions instead of creating more.

- Measurable: Include dates, exact financial numbers, and amounts. Your goal shouldn't be "Make more money"; it should state a specific amount by a particular time.

- Attainable: Your goal must be achievable. You should be able to accomplish it within the constraints of time, money, and environment, as well as your skills and abilities and other essential factors.

- Relevant: Goals should be in line with the direction that you're heading. Keep your goals aligned with your vision, and don't waste time with irrelevant goals that distract you from your real purpose.

- Time bound: Always set specific deadlines for the completion of your goal. Creating a target deadline creates accountability and gives you more motivation to keep moving forward.

- Example of a SMART goal: to weigh 115 pounds by December 31, 2019

- Create affirmations for each one of your goals or desires (see chapter 12 on how to write affirmations). It is best to work with two to three goals at one time.

  - Repeat affirmations three times per day. The best times are first thing in the morning, in the middle of the day, and before bedtime.

  - When you repeat your affirmation, also visualize experiencing what the affirmation describes. See the scene as you would see it if you were looking out at it through your eyes, as if it were happening around you. Use the manifesting meditation described in chapter 12.

- – I have found that listening to sounds like the ones found on http://bit.ly/DrToniHemi-Sync, while I visualize, help sets my brain at a place where I can manifest faster.

- Believe it is possible.

- Release your fears and act when opportunities show up. Things won't show up by magic; you need to take steps to make things happen, and the spirit/universe will provide the necessary resources/inspiration to make it happen.

- Ask for and respond to feedback. Feedback is essential for us to know if we are on track or if we need to change directions.

- Practice persistence with patience.

- Practice gratitude and uncommon appreciation.

Since this is not a book focused on manifesting, I will not go into detail on how to do it. For more information on manifesting, visit my website at https://www.DrToniCamacho.com.

The purpose of this book and this chapter is for you to know the role of your beliefs in manifesting and find ways to rewrite your limiting beliefs. If you have negative ideas in your subconscious, they'll leave you vibrating at a low frequency that isn't conducive to creating your best life. Therefore, to manifest greatness, all you must do is incorporate these principles into your life. Clear all the energy blocks in your energetic anatomy, and change your beliefs with the tools discussed in chapter 12. Always remember that it is not about perfection; it is about practicing every day. Stay committed to the process, and trust that you're exactly where you need to be and that what you desire is on its way.

APPENDIX A

Mindfulness Meditation

This meditation can be done standing up or sitting down, at any time and in any place. All you have to do is be still and focus on your breath for one minute.

Start by breathing in and out slowly. One breath cycle should last for approximately four to six seconds. Breathe in through your nose and out through your mouth, letting your breath flow effortlessly in and out of your body. Purposefully watch your breath, focusing your sense of awareness on its pathway as it enters your body and exits the body and dissipates into the world.

Let go of any thoughts that come. Let go of things you have to do later today or pending work that needs your attention. Simply focus on your breath when you notice that you are thinking and no longer focused. Say the word *thinking*. Let go of the thought without any judgement or condemnation of the experience. Stay with whatever feeling arises, and go back to focusing on the breath.

In the advanced version of this exercise, when you notice that you are thinking, let go of the thought and connect with the emotion, the feeling. Process the emotion and ask yourself, "Who am I without these thoughts?"

It is important to note that mindfulness meditation is not about escaping, ignoring, or repressing negative emotions. Many people, including long-time practitioners of mediation, use meditation as a form of escaping difficult emotions. Meditation is about being present and experiencing whatever emotion arises, without judgement and without chasing thoughts (rumination). It is about building awareness, feeling, and letting go of the judgment.

APPENDIX B

Recommended Reading

- Anatomy of the Spirit by Carolyn Myss

- Ayurveda: The science of Self-healing by Dr. V. Lad

- Ayurveda: A Life of Balance by Maya Tiwari

- Eastern body western mind by Anodea Judith

- Emotional-Spiritual Energies by Berry Kapke

- Get over it by Iyanla Vanzant

- Kundalini and the Chakras by Genevieve Lewis Paulson

- Molecules of Emotions by Candance B. Pert, Ph.D.

- Mudras for Awakening the Energy Body by Alison Denicola.

- The energetics of foods by Steve Gagné

- The emotional code by Bradley Nelson

- The heart and soul of EFT and beyond by Phillip and Jane Mountrose.

- The path of energy by Dr. Synthia Andrews, ND

- The spontaneous healing of belief by Gregg Braden

- The tapping solution by Nick Ortner

- The wheels of life: A user's guide to the chakra system by Anodea Judith, Ph.D.

- Taoist Sexual Secrets by Lee Holden

- Urban Tantra – Sacred sex for the twenty-first century by Barbara Carrellas

- Jewel in the Lotus – the tantric path to higher consciousness by Sunyata Saraswati and Bodhi Avinasha

APPENDIX C

Meridian Stretches

Meridian stretching is a method developed by Shiatsu therapist, Shizuto Masunaga. It is a yoga-like system, with a vast array of movements and stretches to be practiced to use them to restore balance and circulation of energy in the body.

These stretches tonify each meridian pair and improve organ function, energy flow, and emotions. The goal is to relieve tightness, not to force yourself beyond what is comfortable and then feel pain. The more you practice, the more comfortable they become and the higher the effect on well-being and disease prevention.

Wood Element

Liver and Gall bladder meridians

Gall Bladder
1. Bend sideways to the right
2. Switch arms and bend sideways to the left.

Water Element

Kidney and Bladder Meridians

Liver
1. Interlace fingers of both hands together and turn hands so palms face outwards.
2. Bend forward from the hips as you extend arms forward

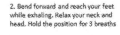

2. Bend forward and reach your feet while exhaling. Relax your neck and head. Hold the position for 3 breaths

1. Inhale

Metal Element

Lungs and Large intestine meridians

2. Inhale

3. Exhale as you bend forward from the hip. Extend your arms up, pointing to the sky with your index finger

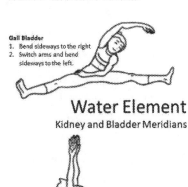

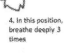

1. Hook up thumbs and extend index fingers

4. In this position, breathe deeply 3 times

Fire Element

Pericardium and triple heater meridians

1. Inhale,
   a) Cross right leg on the inside and left on the outside.
   b) Cross right arm underneath left arm

2. Exhale while bending forward from the hips. When you reach a comfortable stretch, hold the position for 3 breaths.

3. Repeat exercise from the start, crossing arms and legs in the opposite way.

Stomach and Small Intestine Meridians

1. Put the soles feet facing each other. Relax your knees and hips. Inhale

2. Bend forward on exhaling. When you reach a comfortable stretch, hold the positions for 3 breaths.

Earth Element

Stomach and Spleen Meridians

1. Inhale, relaxing your head back.

2. Exhale as you lift your hips up. Hold this position for 3 breaths into the abdomen.

3. You can stretch more by leaning on your elbows for another 3 breaths.

RESOURCES

- For the best hypnotherapy recording visit the Learning strategies website www.Paraliminal.com?aff=1aff145719 or https://www.learningstrategies.com?aff=1aff45719 use this links for special discounts.

- For the best guided meditations to promote energy clearing or manifesting visit: http://bit.ly/DrToniHemi-Sync. Use this link for BEST prices.

- To learn more about QiGong visit Lee Holen's YouTube channel and his website: http://www.leeholden.com/

- One of my favorite binaural beats music is created by The Monroe Institute. You can learn more about it at: http://bit.ly/DrToniHemi-Sync Use this link for BEST prices.

- EFT resources include Nick Ortner www.thetapping solution.com

- Learn how to manifest visit my website. www.drToniCamacho.com Download FREE eBooks at https://www.drtonicamacho.com/free-resources.html

- To buy flower essence formulas visit my website at: http://bit.ly/DrToniFlowerEssences

- To buy Ho'oponopono clearing flower essence visit my website: http://bit.ly/ClearNowFlowerEssence.

Claim your 10% discount

**Discover the Path to Living the
Life of Your Dreams NOW!**

I Can Help you Take your Personal and Career Life to the Next Level. It does not matter whether they are to lose weight, reduce stress, double your income, double your free time or have more balance and fun in your life!

Learn more at www.drToniCamacho.com

Email me the receipt for this book at support@drToniCamacho.com and receive 10% off coupon of your entire order+.

+Offer is limited to www.DrToniCamacho.com website products and services. Affiliate products are excluded.

Need Flower Essences?

**Be Clear NOW! Eliminate Limiting Beliefs
with the Help of Flower Essences**

Flower essences offer a unique and specialized form of subtle energetic therapy. Flower essences are pure and harmless water-soluble drops administered under the tongue, or added to a glass of water, juice, or tea. Do you want to improve your Self-Love/Self-Esteem? Do you want to feel good and attract only good? We provide solutions to both of these questions with our unique and natural flower essences.

Learn more at http://bit.ly/DrToniFlowerEssences

Claim your 10% discount

Email me the receipt for this book at support@drToniCamacho. com and receive 10% off coupon of your entire order+.

Download Free eBooks & Other Resources

Take Back Control of Your Life FREE Workbook

I've prepared a free 14-Day Workbook with simple assignments designed to keep you focused on your goals, while you up level every area of your life. Download now!

For this eBook and other **FREE** resources, visit: https://www.drtonicamacho.com/free-resources.html

REFERENCES

1. *Production of the Threshold Levels of Conscious Sensation By Electrical Stimulation of Human Somatosensory Cortex.* Libet B, Alberts WW, Wright EW Jr, Delattre LD, Levin G, Feinstein B. Jul 1964, Journal of Neurophysiology, Vol. 27, pp. 546-78. 14194958.
2. *The biological function of consciousness.* 697, 8 5, 2014, Frontiers in Psychology, Vol. 5. 25140159.
3. *Wigner's friend, his story.* Mackintosh, R.S. Milton Keynes: s.n., 03 04, 2019, School of Physical Sciences, The Open University.
4. *Operator-Related Anomalies in a Random Mechanical Cascade.* Brenda J. Dunne, Roger D. Nelson, and Robert G. Jahn. 2, s.l.: Pergamon Press, 1998, Journal of Scientific Exploration, Vol. 2, pp. 155-179. 0892-3310/88.
5. *Variance effects in REG series score distributions. (Technical Note PEAR 8500 1).* Jahn, R. G., Nelson, R. D., & Dunne, B. J. New York and London: Princeton Engineering Anomalies Research, Princeton University, School of Engineering/Applied Science, 1985, Natural Inheritance.
6. *Exploratory Study: The Random Number Generator and Group Meditation.* Patterson, Lynne I. Mason and Robert P. 2, Petaluma: s.n., 2007, Journal of Scientific Exploration, Vol. 21, pp. 295-317. 0892-3310/07.
7. *Consciousness and the double-slit interference pattern: Six experiments.* Radin, Dean & Michel, Leena & Galdamez, Karla & Wendland, Paul & Rickenbach, Robert & Delorme, Arnaud. 2, June 2012, Physics Essays, Vol. 25, pp. 157-171.
8. Mermin, M. *Boojums All the Way Through: Communicating Science in a Prosaic Age.* Cambridge: Cambridge University Press, 1990.
9. *Field Effects of Consciousness and Reduction in US Urban Murder Rates: Evaluation of a Prospective, Quasi-Experiment.* Dillbeck, Kenneth L. Cavanaugh and Michael C. 4, Fairfield, Iowa: Institute of Science, Technology, and Public Policy, Maharishi University of Management, 1998, The Journal of Mind and Behavior, Vol. 9, pp. 457-485.

10.   *Psychokinetic Action of Young Chicks on the Path of An Illuminated Source.* Peoc'h, Rene. 1995, Journal of Scientific Exploration, Vol. 2, pp. 223-229. 0892-3310/95.

11.   *Event Perception: A Mind/Brain Perspective.* Jeffrey M. Zacks, Nicole K. Speer, Khena M. Swallow, Todd S. Braver, and Jeremy R. Reynolds. 2, 2007, Psychological bulletin, Vol. 133, pp. 273-293.

12.   Simons, Christopher F. Chabris and Daniel J. *The Invisible Gorilla:.* New York: Broadway Paperback, an inprint of Crown Publishing Group and Division of Random House, 2009.

13.   Center on the Development Child - Harvard University. What Is Early Childhood Development? A Guide to the Science. *Harvard University.* [Online] [Cited: 04 19, 2019.] https://developingchild.harvard.edu/guide/what-is-early-childhood-development-a-guide-to-the-science/.

14.   Hal Stone Ph.D. and Sidra Winkelman, Ph.D. Embracing Each Other - Relationship as Teacher, Healer, and Guide. Mill Valley: Nataraj Publishing, 1989.

15.   Patent, Arnold. *You Can Have it All.* New York: Beyond Words Publishing a Division of Simon and Schuster, Inc, 1995.

16.   Hicks, Esther and Jerry. How to make your relationships better. *Heal Your Life.* [Online] HayHouse, 03 18, 2014. [Cited: 03 05, 2019.] https://www.healyourlife.com/how-to-make-your-relationships-better.

17.   Ruby, Margaret. *The DNA of Healing - A Five Step Pricess for Total Wellness and Abundance.* Charlottesville: Hampton Roads Publishing Company, Inc., 2006.

18.   *Maternal stress in pregnancy: Considerations for fetal development.* DiPietro, Janet A. 2, 2013, The Journal of Adolenscent Health, Vol. 51, pp. 3-8.

19.   Association for Psychological Science. Change in Mother's Mental State Can Influence Her Baby's Development Before and After Birth. [Online] [Cited: 04 18, 2019.] https://www.psychologicalscience.org/news/releases/a-fetus-can-sense-moms-psychological-state.html.

20.   *Impact of Maternal Stress, Depression & Anxiety on Fetal Neurobehavioral Development.* Michael T. Kinsella, B.A. and Catherine Monk, Ph.D. s.l.: Clinical obstetrics and gynecology, Jul 14, 2013, pp. 425-440. 19661759.

21.   Braden, Gregg. The Spontaneous Healing of Belief - Shattering the Paradigm of False Limits. s.l.: HayHouse, Inc., 1997, pp. 91-94.

22. Myss, Carolin. *Anatomy of the Spirit*. New York: Penguin Random House LLC, 1996.

23. *Modulation of muscle responses evoked by transcranial magnetic stimulation during the acquisition of new fine motor skills*. Pascual-Leone A, Nguyet D, Cohen LG, Brasil-Neto JP, Cammarota A, Hallett M. 3, Sep 1995, Neurophysiology, Vol. 74, pp. 1037-45.

24. *From mental power to muscle power–gaining strength by using the mind*. Ranganathan VK, Siemionow V, Liu JZ, Sahgal V, Yue GH. 7, 2004, Neuropsychologia, Vol. 42, pp. 944-56. 14998709.

25. *Kinesthetic imagery training of forceful muscle contractions increases brain signal and muscle strength*. Wan X. Yao, 1,† Vinoth K. Ranganathan, Didier Allexandre, Vlodek Siemionow, and Guang H. Yue. 2013, Frontiers in Human Neuroscience, Vol. 7, p. 561. 24133427.

26. Vitale, Joe and Dr. Hew Len. *Zero Point*. Hoboken: John Wiley and Sons, Inc., 2007.

27. Robert O. Becker MD, and Gary Selden. *The Body Electric*. New York: William Morrow and Company, Inc., 1985. ISBN: 0-688-06971-1.

28. Schiefelbein, Susan. Growing New Limbs. *The Washington Post*. [Online] Saturday Review magazine, August 6, 1978. [Cited: 4 18, 2019.] https://www.washingtonpost.com/archive/opinions/1978/08/06/growing-new-limbs/7dd8603d-6e64-4727-8d1b-47dfa8162478/?noredirect=on&utm_term=.56014c631625.

29. *Movie New Eye of Microscope in War on Germs*. Popular Science. 6, s.l.: Popular Science, 1931, Vol. 118, pp. 27-141.

30. *Observations On Bacillus Typhosus In Its Filterable State: A Preliminary Communication*. Kendall, Arthur Isaac, MD., PhD. and Rife, Royal, PhD. 6, s.l.: California and Western Medicine, 12 1931, Vol. 35, pp. 409-11. 18741967.

31. B, Nordenstrom. *Closed Electric Circuits*. Stockholm: Sweden: Nordic Medical, Publications, 1983.

32. Pitchford, Paul. *Healing with Whole Foods*. Berkeley, Ca.: North Atlantic Books, 2002.

33. Hawkins, David. *Power vs. Force - The Hidden Determinants of Human Behavior*. s.l.: HayHouse, Inc, 2014. 9781401945077.

34. *Effects of Constructive Worry, Imagery Distraction, and Gratitude Interventions on Sleep Quality: A Pilot Trial*. Digdon, N., Koble A. May 2011, Applied Psychology: Health and Wellbeing.

35.   *Examining the Pathways between Gratitude and Self-Rated Physical Health across Adulthood.* Hill PL1, Allemand M, Roberts BW. Jan 2013, Journal of the International Society for the Study of Individual Differences (ISSID), pp. 92-96.

36.   *Gratitude and hedonic and eudaimonic well-being in Vietnam war veterans.* Kashdan TB1, Uswatte G, Julian T. Feb 2006, Behavior Research and Therapy, pp. 177-99.

37.   *What good are positive emotions in crisis? A prospective study of resilience and emotions following the terrorist attacks on the United States on September 11th, 2001.* Fredrickson, B. L., Tugade, M. M., Waugh, C. E., & Larkin, G. R. 2003, Journal of Personality and Social Psychology, pp. 365-376.

38.   *A pilot randomized study of a gratitude journaling intervention on HRV and inflammatory biomarkers in Stage B heart failure patients.* Redwine, L., Henry, B. L., Pung, M. A., Wilson, K., Chinh, K., Knight, B., Mlls, P.J. 2016, Psychosomatic Medicine, pp. 667-676.

39.   *Improving mental health in health care practitioners: randomized controlled trial of a gratitude intervention.* Cheng ST, Tsui PK, Lam JH. s.l.: PsychInfo Database, Sep 15, 2014, pp. 177-86.

40.   Emmons, Robert A. *The little book of gratitude.* Great Britain: Gaia Books, 2016.

41.   Carrellas, Barbara. *Urban Tantra - Sacred Sex for the Twenty-first Century.* New York: Celestial Arts, 2007. 9781587612909.

42.   *Effects of forest environments on blood glucose.* Ohtsuka, Yoshinori. New York: In Forest Medicine, 2003, NOVA Biomedical, pp. 111-116.

43.   Arvay, Clemens. *The Biophilia Effect - A Scientific and Spiritual Exploration of the Healing Bond Between Humans and Nature.* s.l.: Sounds True, 2018.

44.   *Effect of the forest environment on physiological relaxation using the results of field tests at 35 sites throughout Japan.* Park, Bum-Jin & Tsunetsugu, Y & Lee, Juyoung & Kagawa, Takahide & Miyazaki, Yoshifumi. 2013, Forest Medicine, pp. 57-67.

45.   *Subtle Energies and Energy Medicine.* PhD, Elmer E. Green. 4, Vol. 10, p. 368.

46.   PhD, Blair Justice. *Who Gets Sick.* Texas: Peak Press, 2000. 978-0960537624.

47.   HeartMath Institute. Heart Brain Interactions. *HeartMath Institute.* [Online] Oct 2012. [Cited: April 12, 2019.] https://www.

heartmath.org/articles-of-the-heart/the-math-of-heartmath/heart-brain-interactions/.

48.   Harvard Health Publishing. Harvard Medical School. *Uncovering the link between emotional stress and heart disease.* [Online] 04 2017. [Cited: 04 18, 2019.] https://www.health.harvard.edu/heart-disease-overview/uncovering-the-link-between-emotional-stress-and-heart-disease.

49.   WebMD. WebMD. *Many Emotions Can Damage the Heart.* [Online] 2005. [Cited: 04 18, 2019.] https://www.webmd.com/depression/features/many-emotions-can-damage-heart#1.

50.   Lipton, Bruce. *The Biology of Belief.* s.l.: HayHouse, 2005.

51.   Harvard Medical School. The power of the placebo effect. *Harvard Health Publishing.* [Online] 05 2017. https://www.health.harvard.edu/mental-health/the-power-of-the-placebo-effect.

52.   *Antidepressants and the Placebo Effect.* Kirsch, Irving. 3, 2014, Z. Psychology, Vol. 222, pp. 128-134. 25279271.

53.   *A Randomized Trial of Arthroscopic Surgery for Osteoarthritis of the Knee.* Kirkley A, Birmingham TB, Litchfield RB, Giffin JR, Willits KR, Wong CJ, Feagan BG, Donner A, Griffin SH, D'Ascanio LM, Pope JE, Fowler PJ. Sep 11, 2008, New England Journal of Medicine, Vol. 359, pp. 1097-1107.

54.   *A psychosomatic study of contagious dermatitis.* Ikemi Y, Nakagawa S. 1962, Journal of Medical Science, Vol. 13, pp. 335-350.

55.   Jung, Carl. *The Archetypes and the Collective Unconscious.* 2nd. s.l.: Princeton University Press, 1968. Vol. 9.

56.   *George Goodheart, Jr., D.C., and a history of applied kinesiology.* Los Angeles College of Chiropractic, Whittier, California, USA. 5, June 1997, Journal of Manipulative Physiological Therapeutics, Vol. 20, pp. 331-7. 9200049.

57.   Dimond, John. *The Collected Papers of John Diamond, M.D.* s.l.: Enhancement Books, 1980. ISBN 978-1890995300.

58.   *Transcriptional Changes in Cancer Cells Induced by Exposure to a Healing Method.* Sarah Beseme, William Bengston, Dean Radin, Michael Turner, John McMichael. July 11, 2018, SAGE Journals.

59.   *Clinical Studies of Biofield Therapies: Summary, Methodological Challenges, and Recommendations.* Shamini Jain, PhD, corresponding author Richard Hammerschlag, PhD, Paul Mills, PhD, Lorenzo Cohen, PhD, Richard Krieger, MD, Cassandra Vieten,

PhD, and Susan Lutgendorf, PhD. Nov 4, 2015, Global Advances in Health and Medicine, Vol. 4, pp. 58-66.

60. Watkins, Jack Canfield and D.D. *Key to Living the Law of Attraction*. Deerfield Beach: Health Communications. Inc., 2004.

61. Gagne, Steve. *Food Energetics - The Spiritual, Emotional, and Nutritional Power of What we Eat*. Rochester: Healing Arts Press, 1990.

62. *Application of Sound Frequencies as an Epigenetic Tool in Reversing the Limiting Symptoms of Autism*. Kandaswamy, Rajalakshmi. 1, s.l.: Journal of Clinical Epigenetics, 02 13, 2017, Vol. 3.

63. ScienceDaily. Healing Value Of Magnets Demonstrated In Biomedical Engineering Study. *ScienceDaily*. [Online] Jan 7, 2008. [Cited: 04 15, 2019.] https://www.sciencedaily.com/releases/2008/01/080103132307.htm.

64. *Meditation experience is associated with increased cortical thickness*. Sara W. Lazar, a Catherine E. Kerr, b Rachel H. Wasserman, a, b Jeremy R. Gray, c Douglas N. Greve, d Michael T. Treadway, a Metta McGarvey, e Brian T. Quinn, d Jeffery A. Dusek, f, g Herbert Benson, f, g Scott L. Rauch, a Christopher I. Moore, h, i and Bruce Fischld, j. 17, Nov 28, 2005, Neuroreport, Vol. 16, pp. 1893-1897. 16272874.

65. *The influences of chan-chuang qi-gong therapy on complete blood cell counts in breast cancer patients treated with chemotherapy*. M.L. Yeh, T.I. Lee, H.H. Chen, T.Y. Chao. 2, 2006, Cancer Nurs, Vol. 29, pp. 149-155.

66. *Multi-sensory Gamma Stimulation Ameliorates Alzheimer's-Associated Pathology and Improves Cognition*. Anthony J. Martorell, Abigail L. Paulson, Ho-Jun Suk, Fatema Abdurrob, Gabrielle T. Drummond, Webster Guan, Jennie Z. Young, David Nam-Woo Kim, Oleg Kritskiy, Scarlett J. Barker, Vamsi Mangena, Stephanie M. Prince, Emery N. Brown, Kwanghun Chung, Edward S. 2, 03 14, 2019, Cell, Vol. 177, pp. 256-271.

67. *Chemical elemental analysis of single acoustic-levitated water droplets by laser-induced breakdown spectroscopy*. Victor Contreras, Ricardo Valencia, Jairo Peralta, H. Sobral, M. A. Meneses-Nava, Horacio Martinez. s.l.: Science Daily, May 3, 2018, Optics Letters, Vol. 43, p. 2260.

68. Goldman, Jonathan. Sound and the Chakras. *Healing Sounds*. [Online] [Cited: 4 15, 2019.] https://www.healingsounds.com/sound-and-the-chakras/.

69. *Oxytocin Increases Generosity in Humans*. Zak, Stanton &Ahmadi. Claremont Graduate University: PLoS ONE Journal, 2007, California Center for Neuroeconomics Studies and Department of Economics.

70. *The Effects of Environmental Toxins on Allergic Inflammation*. Yang, S.-N., Hsieh, C.-C., Kuo, H.-F., Lee, M.-S., Huang, M.-Y., Kuo, C.-H., & Hung, C.-H. 2014, Allergy, Asthma & Immunology Research, Vol. 6(6), pp. 478–484.

71. *Regret intensity, diurnal cortisol secretion, and physical health in older individuals: Evidence for directional effects and protective factors*. Wrosch, C., Bauer, I., Miller, G. E., & Lupien, S. 2007, Psychology and Aging, Vol. 22, pp. 319-330.

72. WorldOmeters. *The United States Population (Live)*. [Online] Department of Economic and Social Affairs, Population Division, 05 30, 2018.

73. Wilson, James L. *Adrenal Fatigue - The 21ˢᵗ Century Stress Syndrome*. Petaluma: Smart Publications, 2001.

74. Weil, Andrew. Attitude is everything with aging. *Andrew Weil Self Healing Newsletter*. [Online] September 2006.

75. Wachtel-Galor S, Benzie IFF. *Herbal Medicine: Biomolecular and Clinical Aspects*. 2ⁿᵈ. s.l.: CRC Press/Taylor & Francis, 2011.

76. *Environmental Triggers and Autoimmunity. Autoimmune Diseases*. Vojdani, A., Pollard, K. M., & Campbell, A. W. 2014, US National Library of Medicine - National Institute of Health, Vol. 798029.

77. *Healthy Happiness*. Veenhoven. 2008, Journal of Happiness Studies, Vol. 9, pp. 449-469.

78. *View Through a Window May Influence Recovery from Surgery*. Ulrich, Roger. New York: s.n., Science, Vol. 224, pp. 420-1.

79. *Evolving strategies for renoprotection: non-diabetic chronic renal disease*. Taal, M.W. and Brenner, B.M. Jul 2001, Current Opinion in Nephrology and Hypertension 10(4), pp. 523 – 31.

80. *Assessment of the health impact of GM plant diets in long-term and multigenerational animal feeding trials: a literature review*. Snell C, Bernheim A, Bergé JB, Kuntz M, Pascal G, Paris A, Ricroch AE. March 2012, Food and Chemical Toxicology, Vols. 50(3-4), pp. 1134-48.

81. *Discovering environmental causes of disease*. SM, Rappaport. Feb 2012, Journal of Epidemiol Community Health, Vol. 66(2), pp. 99-102.

82. Seligman, Martin E.P. *Authentic Happiness: Using the New Positive Psychology to Realize Your Potential for Lasting Fulfillment.* New York: Free Press, 2002.

83. *Glyphosate, pathways to modern diseases II: Celiac sprue and gluten intolerance.* Samsel, A., & Seneff, S. 2013, Interdisciplinary Toxicology, Vol. 6(4), pp. 159–184.

84. Routledge. *From Aristotle to Augustine: Routledge History of Philosophy.* London: s.n., 2003. Vol. 2.

85. *Effect of Dietary Vitamin D and Calcium on the Growth of Androgen-insensitive Human Prostate Tumor in a Murine Model.* RAHUL RAY, MARA BANKS, HILAL ABUZAHRA,1 VIKRAM J. EDDY, KELLY S. PERSONS, M. SCOTT LUCIA, JAMES R. LAMBERT, and MICHAEL F. HOLICK. 2012, Anticancer Research, Vol. 32(3), pp. 727–731.

86. *Nutritional factors in osteoporosis.* R., Swaminathan. Oct-Nov 1999, International Journal of Clinical Practices 53(7), pp. 540 – 548.

87. Ph.D., Graham C.L. Davey. Negative news on TV is increasing, but what are its psychological effects? *Psychology Today.* [Online] https://www.psychologytoday.com/us/blog/why-we-worry/201206/the-psychological-effects-tv-news.

88. *Mental attitudes to cancer: an additional prognostic factor.* Pettingall, K., et. al. s.l.: Lancet, 1990, p. 750.

89. P., Gilbert. *The Compassionate Mind.* s.l.: New Harbinger Publications, Inc., 2009.

90. Norman Shealy M.D., Ph.D. *Life Beyond 100.* London: Pinguin Group, 2005.

91. Neff, Kristin. Self-Compassion - The Proven Power of Being Kind to Yourself. *Self-Compassion - The Proven Power of Being Kind to Yourself.* New York: HarperCollins, 2011.

92. *Outbursts of anger as a trigger of acute cardiovascular events: a systematic review and meta-analysis.* Mostofsky E, Penner EA, Mittleman MA. June 2014, European Heart Journal, Vol. 1;35(21), pp. 1404-10.

93. *Human Fronto-mesolimbic networks guide descisions about charitable donation.* Moll, Krueger, Zahn, Pardini, Oliveira-Souza & Grafman. s.l.: National Institute of Health, 2006.

94. *Infection, vaccines and other environmental triggers of autoimmunity.* Molina V, Shoenfeld Y. s.l.: National Institute of Health - Autoimmunity, 2005, Vol. 38(3), pp. 235-45.

95. Maimes, David Winston and Steven. *Adaptogens - Herbs for Strength, Stamina, and Stress Relief*. Rochester: Healing Arts Press, 2007.

96. Lyubomirsky, Sonja. *The how of happiness: A scientific approach to getting the life you want*. New York: Penguin Press, 2008.

97. *The benefits and costs of frequent positive affect: Does happiness lead to success?* Lyubomirsky, S., King, L. A., & Diener, E. In Press 2005, Psychological Bulletin.

98. *Neuroanatomical Correlates of Religiosity and Spirituality*. Lisa Miller, Ravi Bansal, Priya Wickramaratne, Xuejun Hao, Craig E. Tenke, Myrna M. Weissman, Bradley S. Peterson. 2013, JAMA Psychiatry.

99. *Drinking water exposure to cadmium, an environmental contaminant, results in the exacerbation of autoimmune disease in the murine model.. 2003;188:233–50*. Leffel EK, Wolf C, Poklis A, White KL. 2003, Toxicology, Vol. 188, pp. 233-50.

100. *Study shows compassion meditation changes the brain*. Land. s.l.: University of Wisconsin, 2008.

101. *How are habits formed: Modelling habit formation in the real world*. Lally, Phillippa and Wardle, Cornelia H. M., van Jaarsveld Henry W. W. Potts Jane. 2009, European Journal of Social Psychology.

102. Ladner, Lorne Ph.D. *The Lost Art of Compassion: Discovering the Practice of Happiness in the Meeting of Buddhism and Psychology*. New York: HaperCollins, 2004.

103. *Association of Religious Involvement and Suicide*. Koenig, Harold G. 2016, JAMA Psychiatry.

104. Koblin, Seymour. *Food for Life - Applying Macrobiotic Principles and Practice to Create Vital Health for Body, Mind and Spirit*. San Diego: Soul Star Creations, 1998.

105. Kemerling. *Aristotle: Ethics and the Virtues*. 2001.

106. Keltner, Dacher. Darwin's Touch: Survival of the Kindest. [Online] 2001. http://www.psychologytoday.com/blog/born-be-good/200902/darwins-touch-survival-the-kindest.

107. *A meaningful life is a healthy life: a conceptual model linking meaning and meaning salience to health*. Hooker, S. A., Masters, K. S., & Park, C. L. July 6, 2017, Review of General Psychology. Advance online publication.

108. *Loneliness and social isolation as risk factors for CVD: implications for evidence-based patient care and scientific inquiry*. Holt-Lunstad, J., & Smith, T. B. July 2016, Heart, Vol. 102(13), pp. 987–989.

109. *Hernandez, R., Kershaw, K. N., Siddique, J., Boehm, J. K., Kubzansky, L. D., Diez-Roux, A., ... Lloyd-Jones, D. M. (2015). Optimism and Cardiovascular Health: Optimism and Cardiovascular Health: Multi-Ethnic Study of Atherosclerosis (MESA).* Hernandez, R., Kershaw, K. N., Siddique, J., Boehm, J. K., Kubzansky, L. D., Diez-Roux, A., ... Lloyd-Jones, D. M. s.l.: Health Behavior and Policy Review, 2(1), 2015, pp. 62–73.

110. *Attending religious services linked to longer lives, study shows.* Harvard, Women's Health Watch. 2016: Harvard Health Publishing.

111. Harvard, Kennedy School. *Social Capital Community Benchmark Survey.* 2006.

112. Haidt. *The Happiness Hypothesis.* New York: Basic Books, 2006.

113. *Psychological response to breast cancer and 15 year ourcome.* Green S., et. al. s.l.: Lancet, 1990, pp. 49 - 50.

114. Gary Marcus, Ph.D. Making the Mind. *Boston Review.* December 2013, Vols. December 2003 - January 2014.

115. Gagne, Steve. *The Energetics of Foods.* Rocherster: Healing Arts Press, 1990.

116. *Epigenetic differences arise during the lifetime of monozygotic twins.* Fraga MF, Ballestar E, Paz MF, et al. s.l.: Proceedings of the National Academy of Sciences of the United States of America., 2005, Vol. 102(30), pp. 10604 - 10609.

117. Firestone, Robert W. Ph.D. Psychology Today. *You Don't Really Know Yourself - Examining the persistence of our negative self-identity.* [Online] 1126 2016. https://www.psychologytoday.com/us/blog/the-human-experience/201611/you-dont-really-know-yourself.

118. Feldscher, Karen. High levels of fluorinated compounds have been linked to cancer, hormone disruption. *The Harvard Gazette.* 2016.

119. *Happy People Live Longer: Subjective well-being contributes to health and longevity.* Ed, Diner. 2011, Applied Psychology: Health and Well-being.

120. *Adverse Effects Associated with Protein Intake above the Recommended Dietary Allowance for Adults.* Delimaris, I. 2013, ISRN Nutrition, Vol. 126929.

121. *Positive Emotions in Early Life and Longevity: Findings from the Nun Study.* Deborah D. Danner, David A. Snowdon, and Wallace V. Friesen. Kentucky: s.n., 2000, Personality Processes and Individual Differences.

122. *The mosaic of autoimmunity: the role of environmental factors.* de Carvalho JF1, Pereira RM, Shoenfeld Y. 2009, Front Biosci, Vol. June 1, pp. 501-9.

123. *Buddha's Brain: Neuroplasticity and Meditation.* Davidson, R. J., & Lutz, A. s.l.: IEEE Signal Processing Magazine, Vol. 25(1), pp. 176–174.

124. *The impact of mindfulness-based interventions on symptom burden, positive psychological outcomes, and biomarkers in cancer patients.* Codie R Rouleau, Sheila N Garland, and Linda E Carlson. 2015, Cancer Management and Research, Vol. 7, pp. 121-131.

125. *Attitudes of Hong Kong Chinese to traditional Chinese medicine and Western medicine: Survey and cluster analysis.* Chan M. F. E, Mok Y. S, Wong ST. F, Tong FM. C, Day CC. K, Tang K, Wong D. H. H. 2003, Complement Ther Med, Vol. 11(2), pp. 103-9.

126. Canfield, Jack. Taking Control of the Environments that Control You. *Jack Canfield - Maximizing Your Potential.* [Online] http://jackcanfield. com/blog/taking-control-of-the-environments-that-control-you/.

127. Candice Pert, Ph.D. *Molecules of Emotions.* New York: Touchstone, 1997.

128. *Autoimmunity and the Gut [accessed May 30 2018].* Campbell, Andrew W. 152428, Land O Lakes: s.n., May 2014, Hindawi Publishing Corporation - Autoimmune Diseases, p. 12.

129. *Silicone breast implants and autoimmunity: causation, association, or myth?* Brautbar N, Campbell A, Vojdani A. s.l.: J Biomater Sci Polym, 1995, Vol. 7(2), pp. 133-45.

130. Blair Justice, Ph.D. *Who gets Sick?* Texas: PeAK Press, 2000.

131. *Dietary emulsifiers impact the mouse gut microbiota promoting colitis and metabolic syndrome.* Benoit Chassaing, Omry Koren, Julia K. Goodrich, Angela C. Poole, Shanthi Srinivasan, Ruth E. Ley & Andrew T. Gewirtz. 2015, International Journal of Science, Vol. 519, pp. 92-96.

132. *Emotion suppression and mortality risk over a 12-year follow-up.* Benjamin P. Chapman'Correspondence information about the author Benjamin P. ChapmanEmail the author Benjamin P. Chapman, Kevin Fiscella, Ichiro Kawachi, Paul Duberstein, Peter Muennig. 4, 2013, Journal of Psychosomatic Research, Vol. 75, pp. 381-385.

133. Barry, Michael. *The Forgiveness Project: The Startling Discovery of How to Overcome Cancer, Find Health, and Achieve Peace.* Grand Rapids: Kregel Publications, 2011.

134.   *Complementary and alternative medicine use among adults and children.* Barnes P. M, Bloom B, Nahin R. Nov 5, 2008, CDC National Health Statistics Report, Vol. 12.

135.   Barasch. *The Compassionate Life – Walking the Path of Kindness.* s.l.: Berret-Koehler Publishers, Inc., 2009.

136.   *Psychological and cognitive determinants of mortality: Evidence from a nationally representative sample followed over thirty-five years.* Amelia Karraker, Robert F.Schoeni, Jennifer C. Cornman. November 2015, Social Science & Medicine, Vol. 144, pp. 69-78.

137.   Aihara, Herman. *Acid and Alkaline.* 5th. s.l.: George Ohsawa Macrobiotic, 1986.

138.   *Religion or spirituality has positive impact on romantic/marital relationships, child development, research shows.* (APA), American Psychological Association. 2014, ScienceDaily.

139.   Institute of HeartMath. The Making of Emotions. *Institute of HeartMath - Expanding Heart Connections.* [Online] May 30, 2015. https://www.heartmath.org/articles-of-the-heart/science-of-the-heart/making-emotions/.

140.   —. The Making of Emotions. *Institute of HeartMath.* [Online] https://www.heartmath.org/articles-of-the-heart/science-of-the-heart/making-emotions.

141.   HH The Dalai Lama & Cutler. *The Art of Happiness (Rev. ed.).* New York: Riverhead Books, 1998.

142.   *Self-Esteem and Autonomic Physiology: Parallels Between Self-Esteem and Cardiac Vagal Tone as Buffers of Threat.* Andy Martens, Jeff Greenberg, John J. B. Allen. 4, Nov 2008, Vol. 12, pp. 370-389.

143.   World Health Organization (WHO). *Report of WHO global survey.* Geneva: National Policy on Traditional Medicine and Regulation of Herbal Medicine, 2005.

144.   *Relationship of Credit Attitude and Debt to Self-Esteem and Locus of Control in College-Age Consumers.* Mary Beth Pinto, Phylis M. Mansfield, Diane H. Parente. 3, June 1, 2004, Penn State Erie, Vol. 94, pp. 1405-1418.

145.   National Institute of Healh. *National Center for Complementary and Integrative Health.* [Online] https://nccih.nih.gov/research/statistics/NHIS.

146.   Monsanto & Co's Dirty Little Secret. *Pesticide Action Network - PAM.* [Online]

147. *Mirror Neuron: a neurological approach to empathy.* Rizzolatti & Craighero. 2005, Journal of Neurobiology of Human Values.

148. *Medical error-the third leading cause of death in the US.* Makary MA, Daniel M. May 3, 2016, BMJ.

149. *Medical and Psychology Student's Experiences in Learning Mindfulness: Benefits, Paradoxes, and Pitfalls.* Solhaug I, Eriksen TE, de Vibe M, Haavind H, Friborg O, Sørlie T, Rosenvinge JH. New York: s.n., April 6, 2016, Mindfulness, Vol. Epub 2016, pp. 838-850.

150. Hart. *Living Oneness. Global Oneness Project.* 2005.

151. Derek D. Rucker and Adam D. Galinsky. KelloggInsight. *Desire to Acquire - Powerlessness and compensatory consumption.* [Online] April 5, 2010. https://insight.kellogg.northwestern.edu/article/desire_to_acquire.

152. *Investigating the Effectiveness of an Arts-Based and Mindfulness-Based Group Program for the Improvement of Resilience in Children in Need.* Coholic, Diana & Eys, Mark & Lougheed, Sean. October 2011, Journal of Child and Family Studies, Vol. 21(5).

153. *Highly religious Americans are more satisfied with their family life.* s.l.: Pew Research Center - Religion & Public Life, 2016.

154. *Highly religious Americans are happier and more involved with family but are no more likely to exercise, recycle or make socially conscious consumer choices.* April 2016, Pew Research Center Religion & Public Life.

155. *Death by Medicine.* Gary Null, Ph.D.; Carolyn Dean, M.D., N.D; Martin Feldman, M.D.; Debora Rasio, M.D. 2005, Journal of Orthomolecular Medicine, Vol. 20.

156. The Foundation for Inner Peace. *Course in Miracles.* Mill Valley: s.n., 2007.

157. *Consumption of ultra-processed foods and cancer risk: results from NutriNet-Santé prospective cohort.* 2018, TheBMJ, Vol. 360, p. 322.

158. Centers for Disease Control and Prevention. Chronic Diease Prevention and Health Promotion. [Online] 2017. https://www.cdc.gov/chronicdisease/overview/index.htm.

159. National Institute of Cancer at the National Institutes of Health. Calcium and Cancer Prevention. [Online] 2009. https://www.cancer.gov/about-cancer/causes-prevention/risk/diet/calcium-fact-sheet.

160. HHS (U.S. Department of Health and Human Services Office on Women's Health. *Autoimmune Diseases Fact Sheet.* 2012.

161. *A Randomized Trial of Mindfulness-Based Cognitive Therapy for Children: Promoting Mindful Attention to Enhance Social-Emotional Resiliency in Children.* Semple, Randye J.; Lee, Jennifer; Rosa, Dinelia; Miller, Lisa F. April 2010, Journal of Child and Family Studies, Vol. 19, pp. 218-229.

162. The Power of Positivity. 8 Studies that Show How Consciousness Affects Reality. *The power of positivity.* [Online] https://www.powerofpositivity.com/8-studies-show-consciousness-affects-reality/.

163. HH The Dalai Lama. *(2003). The Compassionate Life.* Massachusetts: Wisdom Publications, Inc., 2003.

Printed in the United States
By Bookmasters